studysync®

Reading & Writing Companion

Getting Along

studysync®

studysync.com

Send all inquiries to:
BookheadEd Learning, LLC
610 Daniel Young Drive
Sonoma, CA 95476

Cover, ©iStock.com/-aniaostudio-, ©iStock.com/Gannet77, ©iStock.com/alexey_boldin, ©iStock.com/skegbydave

5 6 7 8 9 LWI 21 20 19 18 C

STUDENT GUIDE

GETTING STARTED

Welcome to the StudySync Reading and Writing Companion! In this booklet, you will find a collection of readings based on the theme of the unit you are studying. As you work through the readings, you will be asked to answer questions and perform a variety of tasks designed to help you closely analyze and understand each text selection. Read on for an explanation of each section of this booklet.

CORE ELA TEXTS

In each Core ELA Unit you will read texts and text excerpts that share a common theme, despite their different genres, time periods, and authors. Each reading encourages a closer look with questions and a short writing assignment.

1 INTRODUCTION

An Introduction to each text provides historical context for your reading as well as information about the author. You will also learn about the genre of the excerpt and the year in which it was written.

2 FIRST READ

During your first reading of each excerpt, you should just try to get a general idea of the content and message of the reading. Don't worry if there are parts you don't understand or words that are unfamiliar to you. You'll have an opportunity later to dive deeper into the text.

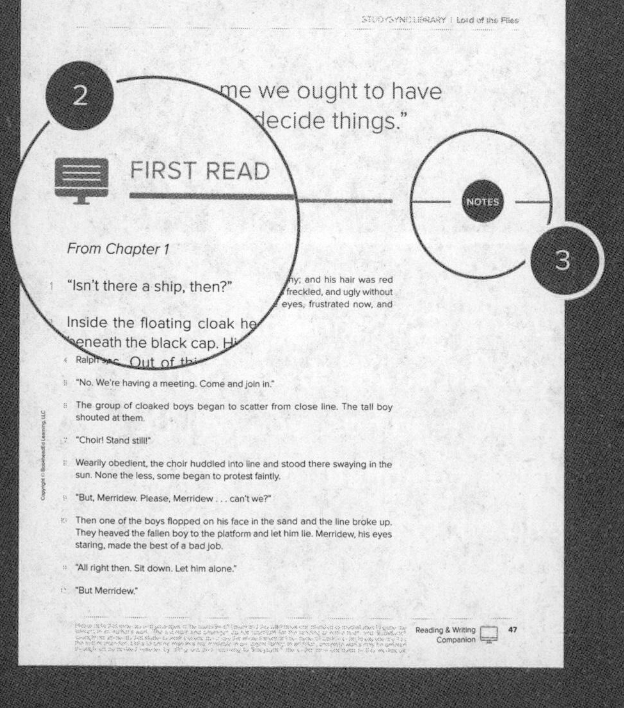

3 NOTES

Many times, while working through the activities after each text, you will be asked to **annotate** or **make annotations** about what you are reading. This means that you should highlight or underline words in the text and use the "Notes" column to make comments or jot down any questions you may have. You may also want to note any unfamiliar vocabulary words here.

4 THINK QUESTIONS

These questions will ask you to start thinking critically about the text, asking specific questions about its purpose, and making connections to your prior knowledge and reading experiences. To answer these questions, you should go back to the text and draw upon specific evidence that you find there to support your responses. You will also begin to explore some of the more challenging vocabulary words used in the excerpt.

5 CLOSE READ & FOCUS QUESTIONS

After you have completed the First Read, you will then be asked to go back and read the excerpt more closely and critically. Before you begin your Close Read, you should read through the Focus Questions to get an idea of the concepts you will want to focus on during your second reading. You should work through the Focus Questions by making annotations, highlighting important concepts, and writing notes or questions in the "Notes" column. Depending on instructions from your teacher, you may need to respond online or use a separate piece of paper to start expanding on your thoughts and ideas.

6 WRITING PROMPT

Your study of each excerpt or selection will end with a writing assignment. To complete this assignment, you should use your notes, annotations, and answers to both the Think and Focus Questions. Be sure to read the prompt carefully and address each part of it in your writing assignment.

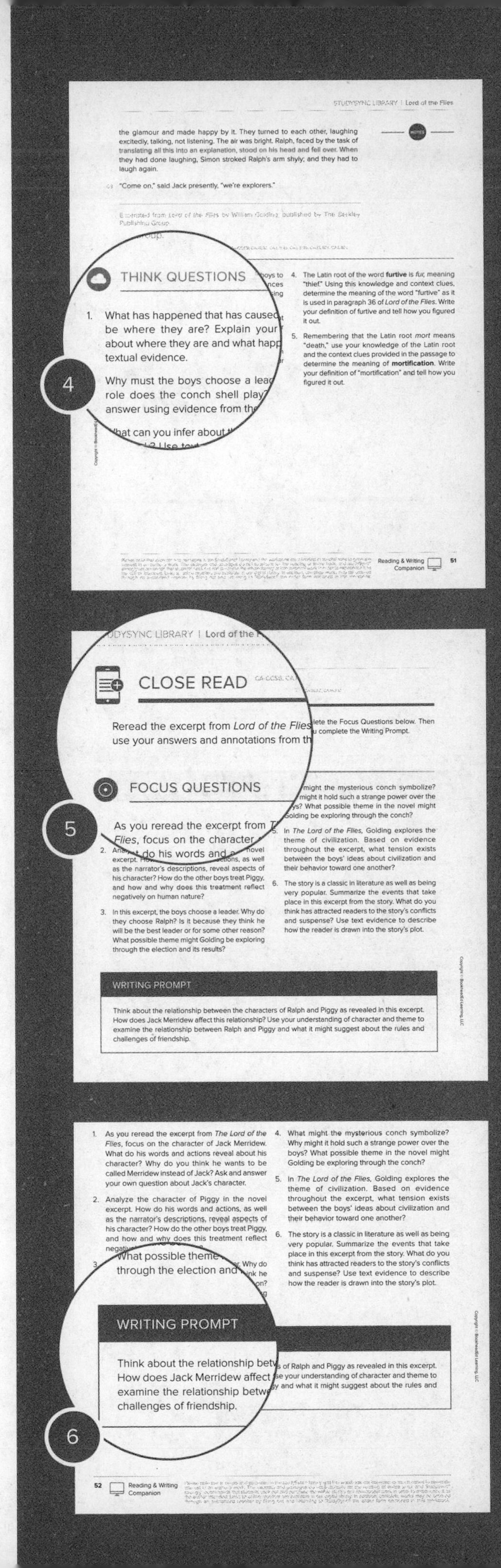

ENGLISH LANGUAGE DEVELOPMENT TEXTS

The English Language Development texts and activities take a closer look at the language choices that authors make to communicate their ideas. Individual and group activities will help develop your understanding of each text.

STUDYSYNC

REREAD

1

Reread paragraphs 8–14 of ... ead, complete the Using Language and Meaningful Interactions activities.

USING LANGUAGE CA-CCSS

The Other Side uses a narrative te... shback. The narrator first describes the present. ...en, the narrator de... s a fla... e past. Finally, the narrator returns to describe the ...t again. The ... paragraphs 1–5 of *The Other Side*. Sort the details

2

Details
The sun took ... t as it had countless times before, our neighborhood slowly came alive.
Now her eyes were begging for help to understand
Something had woken me and I knew that there was no going back to who I had been.
I didn't mention that part when I told Alexandria before
"What aren't you telling me?" she frowned.

First, the narrator describes the present.	Then, the narrator describes the flashback.	Finally, the narrator describes the present again.
I glanced at my sister, Alexandria, swaying under the sycamore tree in our backyard.		

76 Reading & Writing Companion

Copyright © BookheadEd Learning, LLC

... LIBRARY | Sobeknefru

STUDYSYNC

MEANINGFUL INTERACTIONS

Work with your group to discuss the structure of t... fy important events in Sobeknefru's life. The... identify when these events happened. Use ... nes to ask and answer questions during your ... scussion. Last, use the self-evaluation rub... r participation.

- When was Sobeknefru born?

  She was ...

- For how long ... rule Egypt?

  He ruled Egypt . . .

- Who was the pharaoh directly before Sobeknefru?

  The pharaoh directly before Sobeknefru was . . .

- For how long did Sobeknefru rule Egypt?

  She ruled . . .

- When was Amenemhet III's temple finished?

  It was finished . . .

- When did the 12th Dynasty end?

  It ended . . .

3

SELF-ASSESSMENT RUBRIC

	3 I did this well	2 I did this a little bit	1 I did not do this.
I took an active part with my group in doing the assigned tasks.			
I contributed effectively to identify impo...			
I understood ...			
I helped my g... events.			
I used the sentence f... the sequence of ev...			

Copyright © BookheadEd Learning, LLC

1 REREAD

After you have completed the First Read, you will have two additional opportunities to revisit portions of the excerpt more closely. The directions for each reread will specify which paragraphs or sections you should focus on.

2 USING LANGUAGE

These questions will ask you to analyze the author's use of language and conventions in the text. You may be asked to write in sentence frames, fill in a chart, or you may simply choose between multiple-choice options. To answer these questions, you should read the exercise carefully and go back in the text as necessary to accurately complete the activity.

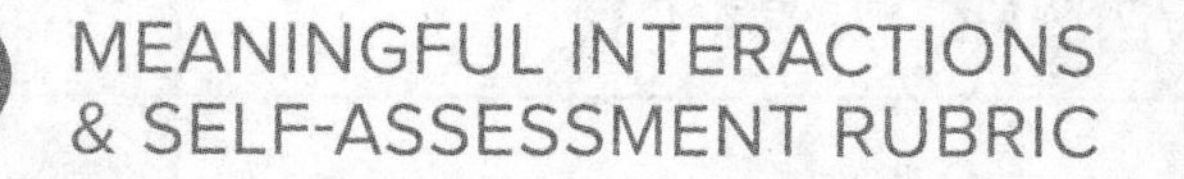

3 MEANINGFUL INTERACTIONS & SELF-ASSESSMENT RUBRIC

After each reading, you will participate in a group activity or discussion with your peers. You may be provided speaking frames to guide your discussions or writing frames to support your group work. To complete these activities, you should revisit the excerpt for textual evidence and support. When you finish, use the Self-Assessment Rubric to evaluate how well you participated and collaborated.

EXTENDED WRITING PROJECT

The Extended Writing Project is your opportunity to explore the theme of each unit in a longer written work. You will draw information from your readings, research, and own life experiences to complete the assignment.

WRITING PROJECT

After you have read all of the unit text selections, you will move on to a writing project. Each project will guide you through the process of writing an argumentative, narrative, informative, or literary analysis essay. Student models and graphic organizers will provide guidance and help you organize your thoughts as you plan and write your essay. Throughout the project, you will also study and work on specific writing skills to help you develop different portions of your writing.

2 WRITING PROCESS STEPS

There are five steps in the writing process: **Prewrite**, **Plan**, **Draft**, **Revise**, and **Edit, Proofread, and Publish**. During each step, you will form and shape your writing project so that you can effectively express your ideas. Lessons focus on one step at a time, and you will have the chance to receive feedback from your peers and teacher.

3 WRITING SKILLS

Each Writing Skill lesson focuses on a specific strategy or technique that you will use during your writing project. The lessons begin by analyzing a student model or mentor text, and give you a chance to learn and practice the skill on its own. Then, you will have the opportunity to apply each new skill to improve the writing in your own project.

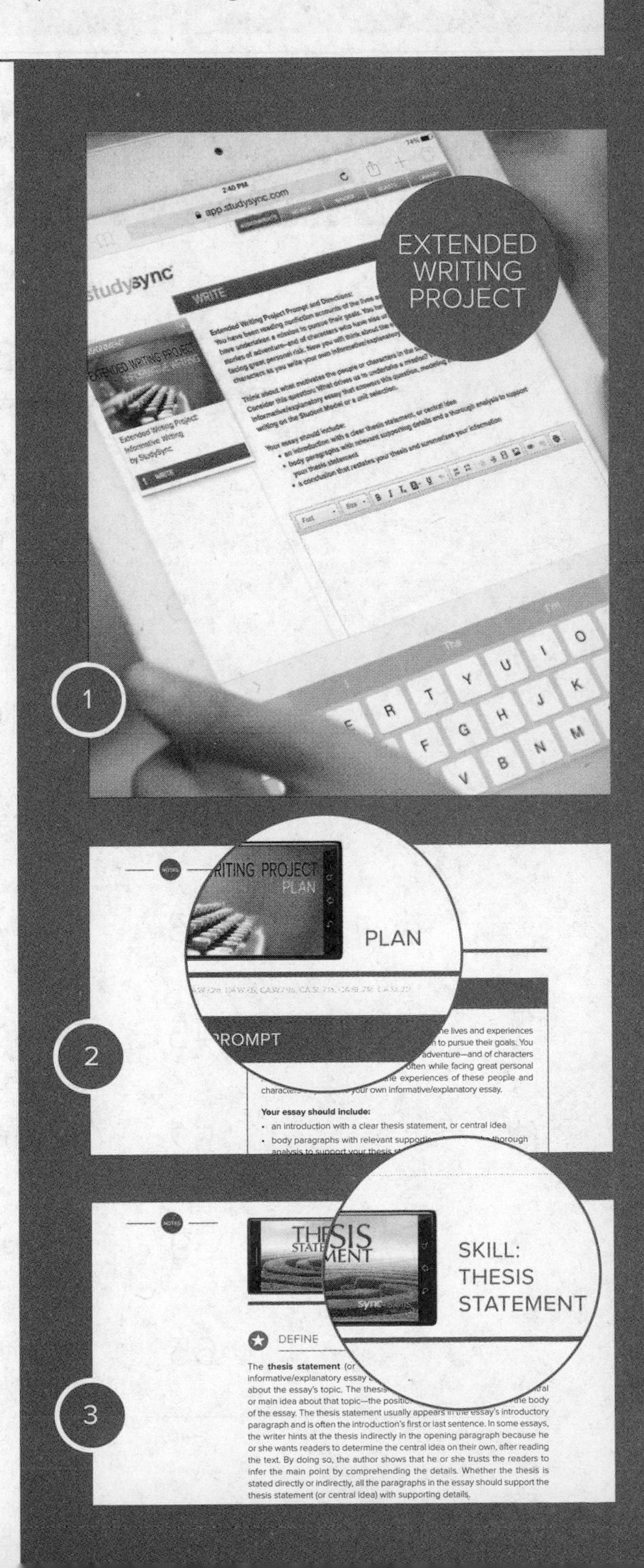

UNIT 4 What are the challenges of human interactions?

Getting Along

TEXTS

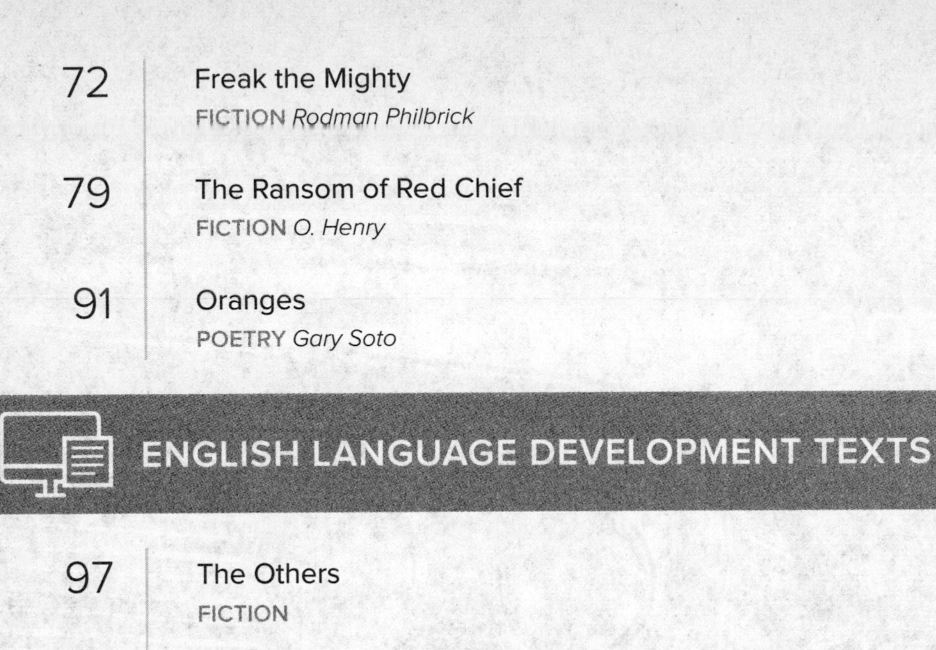

ENGLISH LANGUAGE DEVELOPMENT TEXTS

EXTENDED WRITING PROJECT

THE OUTSIDERS

FICTION

S.E. Hinton

1967

INTRODUCTION

studysync tv

Susan Eloise Hinton was only seventeen years old when her groundbreaking novel *The Outsiders* was first published. Because of the novel's explicit depiction of violence, her publisher believed that the book would do better if the author's gender remained unknown and suggested it be published under her initials. The novel explores the hearts and minds of a gang with no voice, telling the story of class conflict between the lower-class "Greasers" and the upper-class "Socs" (short for "Socials" and pronounced "Soshes") in 1960's middle America. The universal themes transcend both time and location. In the excerpt below from early in the novel, the Greasers learn that the rival Socs have viciously attacked a gang member, Johnny.

"He would carry that scar all his life."

FIRST READ

NOTES

Excerpt from Chapter 2

1 We were used to seeing Johnny banged up—his father clobbered him around a lot, and although it made us madder than heck, we couldn't do anything about it. But those beatings had been nothing like this. Johnny's face was cut up and bruised and swollen, and there was a wide gash from his temple to his cheekbone. He would carry that scar all his life. His white T-shirt was splattered with blood. I just stood there, trembling with sudden cold. I thought he might be dead; surely no one could be beaten like that and live. Steve closed his eyes for a second and muffled a groan as he dropped on his knees beside Soda.

2 Somehow the gang sensed what had happened. Two-Bit was suddenly there beside me, and for once his comical grin was gone and his dancing gray eyes were stormy. Darry had seen us from our porch and ran toward us, suddenly skidding to a halt. Dally was there, too, swearing under his breath, and turning away with a sick expression on his face. I wondered about it vaguely. Dally had seen people killed on the streets of New York's West Side. Why did he look sick now?

3 "Johnny?" Soda lifted him up and held him against his shoulder. He gave the limp body a slight shake. "Hey, Johnnycake."

4 Johnny didn't open his eyes, but there came a soft question. "Soda?"

5 "Yeah, it's me," Sodapop said. "Don't talk. You're gonna be okay."

6 "There was a whole bunch of them," Johnny went on, swallowing, ignoring Soda's command. "A blue Mustang full . . . I got so scared . . ." He tried to swear, but suddenly started crying, fighting to control himself, then sobbing all the more because he couldn't. I had seen Johnny take a whipping with a

NOTES

two-by-four from his old man and never let out a whimper. That made it worse to see him break now. Soda just held him and pushed Johnny's hair back out of his eyes. "It's okay, Johnnycake, they're gone now. It's okay."

7 Finally, between sobs, Johnny managed to gasp out his story. He had been hunting our football to practice a few kicks when a blue Mustang had pulled up beside the lot. There were four Socs in it. They had caught him and one of them had a lot of rings on his hand—that's what had cut Johnny up so badly. It wasn't just that they had beaten him half to death—he could take that. They had scared him. They had threatened him with everything under the sun. Johnny was high-strung anyway, a nervous wreck from getting belted every time he turned around and from hearing his parents fight all the time. Living in those conditions might have turned someone else **rebellious** and bitter; it was killing Johnny. He had never been a coward. He was a good man in a **rumble.** He stuck up for the gang and kept his mouth shut good around cops. But after the night of the beating, Johnny was jumpier than ever. I didn't think he'd ever get over it. Johnny never walked by himself after that. And Johnny, who was the most **law-abiding** of us, now carried in his back pocket a six-inch switchblade. He'd use it, too, if he ever got jumped again. They had scared him that much. He would kill the next person who jumped him. Nobody was ever going to beat him like that again. Not over his dead body. . . .

8 I had nearly forgotten that Cherry was listening to me. But when I came back to reality and looked at her, I was startled to find her as white as a sheet.

9 "All Socs aren't like that," she said. "You have to believe me, Ponyboy. Not all of us are like that."

10 "Sure," I said.

11 "That's like saying all you greasers are like Dallas Winston. I'll bet he's jumped a few people."

12 I digested that. It was true. Dally had jumped people. He had told us stories about muggings in New York that had made the hair on the back of my neck stand up. But not all of us are that bad.

13 Cherry no longer looked sick, only sad. "I'll bet you think the Socs have it made. The rich kids, the West-side Socs. I'll tell you something, Ponyboy, and it may come as a surprise. We have troubles you've never heard of. You want to know something?" She looked me straight in the eye. "Things are rough all over."

14 "I believe you," I said. "We'd better get out there with the popcorn or Two-Bit'll think I ran off with his money."

• • •

NOTES

15 After the movie was over it suddenly came to us that Cherry and Marcia didn't have a way to get home. Two-Bit **gallantly** offered to walk them home—the west side of town was only about twenty miles away—but they wanted to call their parents and have them come and get them. Two-Bit finally talked them into letting us drive them home in his car. I think they were still half-scared of us. They were getting over it, though, as we walked to Two-Bit's house to pick up the car. It seemed funny to me that Socs—if these girls were any example—were just like us. They liked the Beatles and thought Elvis Presley was out, and we thought the Beatles were rank and that Elvis was tuff, but that seemed the only difference to me. Of course greasy girls would have acted a lot tougher, but there was a basic sameness. I thought maybe it was money that separated us.

16 "No," Cherry said slowly when I said this. "It's not just money. Part of it is, but not all. You greasers have a different set of values. You're more emotional. We're **sophisticated**—cool to the point of not feeling anything. Nothing is real with us. You know, sometimes I'll catch myself talking to a girl-friend, and I realize I don't mean half of what I'm saying. I don't really think a beer blast on the river bottom is super-cool, but I'll rave about one to a girl-friend just to be saying something." She smiled at me. "I never told anyone that. I think you're the first person I've ever really gotten through to."

Excerpted from *The Outsiders* by S. E. Hinton, published by the Penguin Group.

THINK QUESTIONS

CA-CCSS: CA.RL.7.1, CA.L.7.4a, CA.L.7.4b, CA.L.7.4c, CA.L.7.4d, CA.L.7.5b, CA.SL.7.1a, CA.SL.7.1c, CA.SL.7.1d, CA.SL.7.2, CA.SL.7.3

1. How did the Greasers react to the beatings Johnny received from his father? What evidence is there in paragraphs 1–5 that the Greasers were more deeply affected by Johnny's beating at the hands of the Socs? Why do you think this was the case? Cite specific evidence from the text to support your response.

2. How did being beaten by the Socs affect Johnny? What about the fight caused this reaction in him? Cite specific evidence from paragraph 7 to support your ideas.

3. What does Ponyboy think separates the Greasers from the Socs? How does Cherry respond to his idea? Cite specific evidence from the text to support your statements.

4. Knowing that the small word rebel is contained in the word **rebellious** in paragraph 7 of *The Outsiders* can help you figure out the meaning of *rebellious*. Use a dictionary to find several meanings for the noun *rebel,* but use only the meaning of *rebel* that will help you determine the meaning of *rebellious* in context. Write your definition of *rebellious* and tell how you figured out its meaning. Refer to the dictionary again to confirm or revise your definition.

5. Use context clues to determine the meaning of the hyphenated compound word **law-abiding** as it is used in paragraph 7 of *The Outsiders*. Write your definition of *law-abiding* and explain how you figured out the meaning of the word. What word or expression might be an antonym for *law-abiding*?

CLOSE READ

CA-CCSS: CA.RL.7.1, CA.RL.7.2, CA.RL.7.6, CA.W.7.2a, CA.W.7.2b, CA.W.7.2c, CA.W.7.2d, CA.W.7.2e, CA.W.7.2f, CA.W.7.4, CA.W.7.5, CA.W.7.6, CA.W.7.9a, CA.W.7.10

Reread the excerpt from *The Outsiders*. As you reread, complete the Focus Questions below. Then use your answers and annotations from the questions to help you complete the Writing Prompt.

FOCUS QUESTIONS

1. As you reread *The Outsiders,* highlight specific textual evidence in paragraphs 1–7 that helped you infer Ponyboy's point of view about the Socs. Make annotations to record your inferences.

2. What textual evidence in paragraphs 9–14 helps you infer that Cherry is beginning to influence Ponyboy's point of view about the Socs? Highlight the textual evidence. Make annotations to support your analysis.

3. In paragraph 15, what evidence is there that Ponyboy's point of view about the Socs is beginning to change? Highlight textual evidence and make annotations to explain your reasoning.

4. In paragraph 16, Cherry says, "You greasers have a different set of values. You're more emotional." In contrast, she says that Socs are "sophisticated—cool to the point of not feeling anything. Nothing is real with us." Highlight textual evidence collected throughout the excerpt that supports Cherry's point of view. Make annotations to explain your choices.

5. Use textual evidence and inferences drawn from *The Outsiders* to describe how this interaction between Ponyboy and Cherry demonstrates that human interactions are challenging. Highlight the specific textual evidence and make annotations to record your inferences.

WRITING PROMPT

Use textual evidence to make three inferences about how interacting with Cherry has changed Ponyboy's point of view about the Greasers and the Socs. Consider which pieces of textual evidence help you make these inferences and how your own prior knowledge supports them. Begin with a clear thesis statement. Use your understanding of textual evidence and point of view to organize and support your writing. Use transitions to show the relationships among your ideas, and provide a conclusion that summarizes your main points.

THE TEACHER WHO CHANGED MY LIFE

NON-FICTION

Nicholas Gage

1989

INTRODUCTION

Author and investigative journalist Nicholas Gage was born in Greece and came to the United States when he was 10. He is perhaps best known for two autobiographical memoirs—*Eleni*, which celebrates his mother's courage for arranging his escape from communist Greece after World War II, and a *A Place for Us*, which narrates his family's experiences as immigrants in the United States in the 1950s. The excerpt here comes from a personal essay first published in *Parade* magazine in 1989. In it, Gage describes his relationship with his junior high school English teacher, and reflects on her lasting influence in his life.

"She was the catalyst that sent me into journalism..."

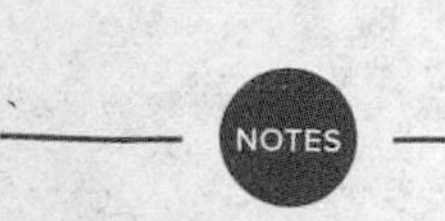

FIRST READ

1 The person who set the course of my life in the new land entered as a young war refugee—who, in fact, nearly dragged me on to the path that would bring all the blessings I've received in America—was a salty-tongued, no-nonsense schoolteacher named Marjorie Hurd. When I entered her classroom in 1953, I had been to six schools in five years, starting in the Greek village where I was born in 1939.

2 When I stepped off a ship in New York Harbor on a gray March day in 1949, I was an undersized 9-year-old in short pants who had lost his mother and was coming to live with the father he didn't know. My mother, Eleni Gatzoyiannis, had been imprisoned, tortured, and shot by Communist **guerrillas** for sending me and three of my four sisters to freedom. She died so that her children could go to their father in the United States.

3 The portly, bald, well-dressed man who met me and my sisters seemed a foreign, authoritarian figure. I secretly resented him for not getting the whole family out of Greece early enough to save my mother. Ultimately, I would grow to love him and appreciate how he dealt with becoming a single parent at the age of 56, but at first our relationship was prickly, full of hostility.

4 As Father drove us to our new home—a tenement in Worcester, Mass.—and pointed out the huge brick building that would be our first school in America, I clutched my Greek notebooks from the refugee camp, hoping that my few years of schooling would impress my teachers in this cold, crowded country. They didn't. When my father led me and my 11-year-old sister to Greendale Elementary School, the grim-faced Yankee principal put the two of us in a class for the mentally retarded. There was no facility in those days for non-English-speaking children.

NOTES

5 By the time I met Marjorie Hurd four years later, I had learned English, been placed in a normal, graded class, and had even been chosen for the college preparatory track in the Worcester public school system. I was 13 years old when our father moved us yet again, and I entered Chandler Junior High shortly after the beginning of the seventh grade. I found myself surrounded by richer, smarter, and better-dressed classmates who looked askance at my strange clothes and heavy accent. Shortly after I arrived, we were told to select a hobby to pursue during "club hour" on Fridays. The idea of hobbies and clubs made no sense to my immigrant ears, but I decided to follow the prettiest girl in my class—the blue-eyed daughter of the local Lutheran minister. She led me through the door marked "Newspaper Club" and into the presence of Miss Hurd, the newspaper adviser and English teacher who would become my **mentor** and my **muse**.

6 A formidable, solidly built woman with salt-and-pepper hair, a steely eye, and a flat Boston accent, Miss Hurd had no patience with layabouts. "What are all you goof-offs doing here?" she bellowed at the would-be journalists. "This is the Newspaper Club! We're going to put out a newspaper. So if there's anybody in this room who doesn't like work, I suggest you go across to the Glee Club now, because you're going to work your tails off here!"

7 I was soon under Miss Hurd's spell. She did indeed teach us to put out a newspaper, skills I honed during my next 25 years as a journalist. Soon I asked the principal to transfer me to her English class as well. There, she drilled us on grammar until I finally began to understand the logic and structure of the English language. She assigned stories for us to read and discuss; not tales of heroes, like the Greek myths I knew, but stories of underdogs—poor people, even immigrants, who seemed ordinary until a crisis drove them to do something extraordinary. She also introduced us to the literary wealth of Greece—giving me a new perspective on my war-ravaged, impoverished homeland. I began to be proud of my origins.

8 One day, after discussing how writers should write about what they know, she assigned us to compose an essay from our own experience. Fixing me with a stern look, she added, "Nick, I want you to write about what happened to your family in Greece." I had been trying to put those painful memories behind me and left the assignment until the last moment. Then, on a warm spring afternoon, I sat in my room with a yellow pad and pencil and stared out the window at the buds on the trees. I wrote that the coming of spring always reminded me of the last time I said goodbye to my mother on a green and gold day in 1948.

9 I kept writing, one line after another, telling how the Communist guerrillas occupied our village, took our home and food, how my mother started planning our escape when she learned the children were to be sent to

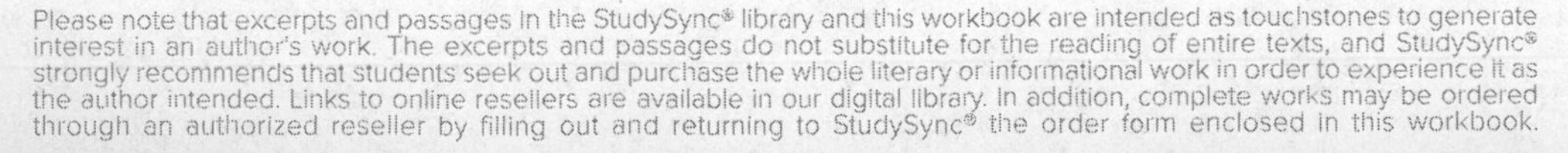

NOTES

reeducation camps behind the Iron Curtain and how, at the last moment, she couldn't escape with us because the guerrillas sent her with a group of women to thresh wheat in a distant village. She promised she would try to get away on her own, she told me to be brave and hung a silver cross around my neck, and then she kissed me. I watched the line of women being led down into the ravine and up the other side, until they disappeared around the bend—my mother a tiny brown figure at the end who stopped for an instant to raise her hand in one last farewell.

10 I wrote about our nighttime escape down the mountain, across the minefields and into the lines of the Nationalist soldiers, who sent us to a refugee camp. It was there that we learned of our mother's execution. I felt very lucky to have come to America, I concluded, but every year, the coming of spring made me feel sad because it reminded me of the last time I saw my mother.

11 I handed in the essay, hoping never to see it again, but Miss Hurd had it published in the school paper. This **mortified** me at first, until I saw that my classmates reacted with sympathy and tact to my family's story. Without telling me, Miss Hurd also submitted the essay to a contest sponsored by the Freedoms Foundation at Valley Forge, Pa., and it won a medal. The Worcester paper wrote about the award and quoted my essay at length. My father, by then a "five-and-dime-store chef," as the paper described him, was ecstatic with pride, and the Worcester Greek community celebrated the honor to one of its own.

12 For the first time I began to understand the power of the written word. A secret ambition took root in me. One day, I vowed, I would go back to Greece, find out the details of my mother's death and write about her life, so her grandchildren would know of her courage. Perhaps I would even track down the men who killed her and write of their crimes. Fulfilling that ambition would take me 30 years.

13 Meanwhile, I followed the literary path that Miss Hurd had so forcefully set me on. After junior high, I became the editor of my school paper at Classical High School and got a part-time job at the Worcester Telegram and Gazette. Although my father could only give me $50 and encouragement toward a college education, I managed to finance four years at Boston University with scholarships and part-time jobs in journalism. During my last year of college, an article I wrote about a friend who had died in the Philippines—the first person to lose his life working for the Peace Corps—led to my winning the Hearst Award for College Journalism. And the plaque was given to me in the White House by President John F. Kennedy.

14 For a refugee who had never seen a motorized vehicle or indoor plumbing until he was 9, this was an unimaginable honor. When the Worcester paper

NOTES

ran a picture of me standing next to President Kennedy, my father rushed out to buy a new suit in order to properly receive the congratulations of the Worcester Greeks. He clipped out the photograph, had it laminated in plastic and carried it in his breast pocket for the rest of his life to show everyone he met. I found the much-worn photo in his pocket on the day he died 20 years later.

15 In our isolated Greek village, my mother had bribed a cousin to teach her to read, for girls were not supposed to attend school beyond a certain age. She had always dreamed of her children receiving an education. She couldn't be there when I graduated from Boston University, but the person who came with my father and shared our joy was my former teacher, Marjorie Hurd. We celebrated not only my bachelor's degree but also the scholarships that paid my way to Columbia's Graduate School of Journalism. There, I met the woman who would eventually become my wife. At our wedding and at the baptisms of our three children, Marjorie Hurd was always there, dancing alongside the Greeks.

16 By then, she was Mrs. Rabidou, for she had married a widower when she was in her early 40s. That didn't distract her from her vocation of introducing young minds to English literature, however. She taught for a total of 41 years and continually would make a "project" of some balky student in whom she spied a spark of potential. Often these were students from the most troubled homes, yet she would alternately bully and charm each one with her own special brand of tough love until the spark caught fire. She retired in 1981 at the age of 62 but still avidly follows the lives and careers of former students while overseeing her adult stepchildren and driving her husband on camping trips to New Hampshire.

17 Miss Hurd was one of the first to call me on Dec. 10, 1987, when President Reagan, in his television address after the summit meetings with Gorbachev, told the nation that Eleni Gatzoyiannis' dying cry, "My children!" had helped inspire him to seek an arms agreement "for all the children of the world."

18 "I can't imagine a better monument for your mother," Miss Hurd said with an uncharacteristic catch in her voice.

19 Although a bad hip makes it impossible for her to join in the Greek dancing, Marjorie Hurd Rabidou is still an honored and enthusiastic guest at all family celebrations, including my 50th birthday picnic last summer, where the shish kebab was cooked on spits, clarinets and bouzoukis wailed, and costumed dancers led the guests in a serpentine line around our Colonial farmhouse, only 20 minutes from my first home in Worcester.

20 My sisters and I felt an aching void because my father was not there to lead the line, balancing a glass of wine on his head while he danced, the way he

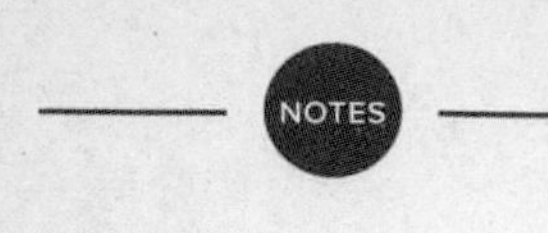

did at every celebration during his 92 years. But Miss Hurd was there, surveying the scene with quiet satisfaction. Although my parents are gone, her presence was a consolation, because I owe her so much.

21 This is truly the land of opportunity, and I would have enjoyed its bounty even if I hadn't walked into Miss Hurd's classroom in 1953. But she was the one who directed my grief and pain into writing, and if it weren't for her, I wouldn't have become an investigative reporter and foreign correspondent, recorded the story of my mother's life and death in Eleni and now my father's story in *A Place for Us,* which is also a testament to the country that took us in. She was the **catalyst** that sent me into journalism and indirectly caused all the good things that came after. But Miss Hurd would probably deny this emphatically.

22 A few years ago, I answered the telephone and heard my former teacher's voice telling me, in that won't-take-no-for-an-answer tone of hers, that she had decided I was to write and deliver the eulogy at her funeral. I agreed (she didn't leave me any choice), but that's one assignment I never want to do. I hope, Miss Hurd, that you'll accept this remembrance instead.

THINK QUESTIONS CA-CCSS: CA.RI.7.1, CA.L.7.4a, CA.L.7.4d

1. Use specific details from the second paragraph to write two or three sentences summarizing why Nicholas Gage came to the United States.

2. Refer to specific details from the text to support your understanding of how Nicholas Gage first met Marjorie Hurd. What does he mean in paragraph 7 when he says, "I was soon under Miss Hurd's spell"?

3. What does Miss Hurd tell Gage to write about? In what way is the assignment a turning point in his life? Cite textual evidence from paragraphs 8–12 to support your response.

4. Use context to determine the meaning of the word **mentor** as it is used in paragraph 5 in "The Teacher Who Changed My Life." Write your definition of *mentor* and tell how you determined its meaning. Check your meaning in context and then confirm it in a print or digital dictionary.

5. Use the context clues provided in the passage to determine the meaning of the word **catalyst** as it is used in paragraph 21 in "The Teacher Who Changed My Life." Write your definition of *catalyst* and tell how you figured out the meaning of the word.

CLOSE READ

CA-CCSS: CA.RI.7.1, CA.RI.7.2, CA.RI.7.3, CA.RI.7.4, CA.W.7.3a, CA.W.7.3b, CA.W.7.3c, CA.W.7.3d, CA.W.7.3e, CA.W.7.4, CA.W.7.5, CA.W.7.6, CA.W.7.10, CA.L.7.5c

Reread the text "The Teacher Who Changed My Life." As you reread, complete the Focus Questions below. Then use your answers and annotations from the questions to help you complete the Writing Prompt.

FOCUS QUESTIONS

1. What adjectives does Gage use to describe Marjorie Hurd in paragraph 1? What details does he supply in paragraph 6 that support this view of Miss Hurd? What evidence is there in paragraph 7 that the young Gage was influenced by Hurd's personality? Highlight textual evidence and make annotations to explain your responses.

2. Which details in paragraph 7 indicate how Miss Hurd shaped the author's ideas through her teaching? Highlight textual evidence and make annotations to explain your answer.

3. What evidence is there in paragraph 7 that Miss Hurd's "Newspaper Club" helped prepare the author for a career in journalism? Highlight textual evidence and make annotations to explain your reasoning.

4. In paragraph 21, how does Gage connect events in his life to Miss Hurd's influence? Highlight textual evidence and make annotations to support your analysis.

5. When speaking about his father, the author notes that "at first our relationship was prickly, full of hostility." Cite textual evidence from paragraph 3 to explain why their interaction was challenging at first and what caused it to change. What evidence exists in paragraphs 13 and 14 to support the idea that his father's actions changed the way they interacted with each other? Highlight textual evidence and make annotations to support your reasoning.

WRITING PROMPT

In the first paragraph of Nicholas Gage's personal essay "The Teacher Who Changed My Life," his teacher Marjorie Hurd is identified as the "person who set the course of . . . [his] life," influencing his choice of a career in journalism and shaping other events in his life. Using the excerpt as a model, write a real-life story, or personal narrative, about a time when someone greatly influenced you. What was the situation? Who was involved? What was the setting? Remember that your personal narrative should be told from the first-person ("I") point of view. Write a strong introduction and include a "hook" to engage your reader. Introduce the setting. Then elaborate on your experience in your middle paragraphs. Include descriptive details. Use transitions, or time order words, such as *first, next,* and *then,* to help your readers follow the sequence of events. Include dialogue and precise or sensory language to hold your readers' attention. Try to use words with connotations that support the overall mood and tone of your story. Finally, write a conclusion that summarizes your personal narrative, and tell what you learned from the experience. What theme (or message) might you want to leave with your reader?

THE MIRACLE WORKER

DRAMA

William Gibson
1956

INTRODUCTION

"The Miracle Worker," by playwright William Gibson, was not only an award-winning Broadway play, but also an Academy Award-winning film. Based on the autobiography of Helen Keller, *The Story of My Life*, "The Miracle Worker" presents an emotional account of Keller's early life, after she lost her sight and hearing. The excerpt here comes from Act III of the play, and illustrates the unflagging efforts of teacher Annie Sullivan to break through Helen's walls of darkness and silence. In sharing the story of Helen Keller, who went on to become a world-famous author and political activist, Gibson provides a powerful portrait of two strong-willed females whose success was guided by their spirit of determination.

"...teaching her is bound to be painful, to everyone."

FIRST READ

CHARACTERS:

ANNIE SULLIVAN: young teacher trained to work with the blind and deaf; in her early twenties
HELEN KELLER: child who has been blind and deaf since infancy; now seven years old
KATE KELLER: Helen's mother; in her early thirties
CAPTAIN KELLER: Helen's father; middle-aged
JAMES KELLER: Captain Keller's grown son by a previous marriage; in his early twenties
AUNT EV: Captain Keller's sister; middle-aged
VINEY: Keller family servant

TIME: *The 1880's.*
PLACE: *In and around the Keller homestead in Tuscumbia, Alabama. . .*

1 [*Now in the family room the rear door opens, and* HELEN *steps in. She stands a moment, then sniffs in one deep grateful breath, and her hands go out vigorously to familiar things, over the door panels, and to the chairs around the table, and over the silverware on the table, until she meets* VINEY; *she pats her flank approvingly.*]

2 VINEY: Oh, we glad to have you back too, prob'ly.

3 [HELEN *hurries groping to the front door, opens and closes it, removes its key, opens and closes it again to be sure it is unlocked, gropes back to the rear door and repeats the procedure, removing its key and hugging herself gleefully.* AUNT EV *is next in by the rear door, with a relish tray; she bends to kiss* HELEN'S *cheek.* HELEN *finds* KATE *behind her, and thrusts the keys at her.*]

NOTES

4 KATE: What? Oh.

5 [*To* EV]

6 Keys.

7 [*She pockets them, lets* HELEN *feel them.*]

8 Yes, *I'll* keep the keys. I think we've had enough of locked doors, too.

9 [JAMES, *having earlier put* ANNIE'S *suitcase inside her door upstairs and taken himself out of view around the corner, now reappears and comes down the stairs as* ANNIE *and* KELLER *mount the porch steps. Following them into the family room, he pats* ANNIE'S *hair in passing, rather to her surprise.*]

10 JAMES: Evening, general.

11 [*He takes his own chair opposite.* VINEY *bears the empty water pitcher out to the porch. The remaining suggestion of garden house is gone now, and the water pump is* ***unobstructed;*** VINEY *pumps water into the pitcher.* KATE *surveying the table breaks the silence.*]

12 KATE: Will you say grace, Jimmie?

13 [*They bow their heads, except for* HELEN, *who palms her empty plate and then reaches to be sure her mother is there.* JAMES *considers a moment, glances across at* ANNIE, *lowers his head again, and obliges.*]

14 JAMES [*Lightly*]: And Jacob was left alone, and wrestled with an angel until the breaking of the day; and the hollow of Jacob's thigh was out of joint, as he wrestled with him; and the angel said, Let me go, for the day breaketh. And Jacob said, I will not let thee go, except thou bless me. Amen.

15 [ANNIE *has lifted her eyes suspiciously at* JAMES, *who winks expressionlessly and inclines his head to* HELEN.]

16 Oh, you angel.

17 [*The others lift their faces;* VINEY *returns with the pitcher, setting it down near* KATE, *then goes out the rear door; and* ANNIE *puts a napkin around* HELEN.]

18 AUNT EV: That's a very strange grace, James.

19 KELLER: Will you start the muffins, Ev?

NOTES

20 JAMES: It's from the Good Book, isn't it?

21 AUNT EV [*Passing a plate*]: Well, of course it is. Didn't you know?

22 JAMES: Yes, I knew.

23 KELLER [*Serving*]: Ham, Miss Annie?

24 ANNIE: Please.

25 AUNT EV: Then why ask?

26 JAMES: I meant it *is* from the Good Book, and therefore a fitting grace.

27 AUNT EV: Well, I don't know about *that.*

28 KATE [*With the pitcher*]: Miss Annie?

29 ANNIE: Thank you.

30 AUNT EV: There's an awful *lot* of things in the Good Book that I wouldn't care to hear just before eating.

31 [*When* ANNIE *reaches for the pitcher,* HELEN *removes her napkin and drops it to the floor.* ANNIE *is filling* HELEN'S *glass when she notices it; she considers* HELEN'S *bland expression a moment, then bends,* ***retrieves*** *it, and tucks it around* HELEN'S *neck again.*]

32 JAMES: Well, fitting in the sense that Jacob's thigh was out of joint, and so is this piggie's.

33 AUNT EV: I declare, James—

34 KATE: Pickles, Aunt Ev?

35 AUNT EV: Oh, I should say so, you know my opinion of your pickles—

36 KATE: This is the end of them, I'm afraid. I didn't put up nearly enough last summer, this year I intend to—[*She interrupts herself, seeing* HELEN ***deliberately*** *lift off her napkin and drop it again to the floor. She bends to retrieve it, but* ANNIE *stops her arm.*]

37 KELLER [*Not noticing*]: Reverend looked in at the office today to complain his hens have stopped laying. Poor fellow, *he* was out of joint, all he could—[*He stops too, to frown down the table at* KATE, HELEN, *and* ANNIE *in turn, all suspended in mid-motion.*]

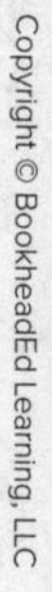

NOTES

38 JAMES [*Not noticing*]: I've always suspected those hens.

39 AUNT EV: Of what?

40 JAMES: I think they're Papist. Has he tried—[*He stops, too, following* KELLER'S *eyes.* ANNIE *now stops to pick the napkin up.*]

41 AUNT EV: James, now you're pulling my—lower extremity, the first thing you know we'll be—

42 [*She stops, too, hearing herself in the silence.* ANNIE, *with everyone now watching, for the third time puts the napkin on* HELEN. HELEN *yanks it off, and throws it down.* ANNIE *rises, lifts* HELEN'S *plate, and bears it away.* HELEN, *feeling it gone, slides down and commences to kick up under the table; the dishes jump.* ANNIE ***contemplates*** *this for a moment, then coming back takes* HELEN'S *wrists firmly and swings her off the chair.* HELEN *struggling gets one hand free, and catches at her mother's skirt; when* KATE *takes her by the shoulders,* HELEN *hangs quiet.*]

43 KATE: Miss Annie.

44 ANNIE: No.

45 KATE [*A pause*]: It's a very special day.

46 ANNIE [*Grimly*]: It will be, when I give in to that.

47 [*She tries to disengage* HELEN'S *hand;* KATE *lays hers on* ANNIE'S.]

48 ANNIE: Captain Keller.

49 KELLER [*Embarrassed*]: Oh, Katie, we—had a little talk, Miss Annie feels that if we **indulge** Helen in these—

50 AUNT EV: But what's the child done?

51 ANNIE: She's learned not to throw things on the floor and kick. It took us the best part of two weeks and—

52 AUNT EV: But only a napkin, it's not as if it were breakable!

53 ANNIE: And everything she's learned *is*? Mrs. Keller, I don't think we should—play tug-of-war for her, either give her to me or you keep her from kicking.

54 KATE: What do you wish to do?

NOTES

55 ANNIE: Let me take her from the table.

56 AUNT EV: Oh, let her stay, my goodness, she's only a child, she doesn't have to wear a napkin if she doesn't want to her first evening—

57 ANNIE [*Level*]: And ask outsiders not to interfere.

58 AUNT EV [*Astonished*]: Out—outsi—I'm the child's aunt!

59 KATE [*Distressed*]: Will once hurt so much, Miss Annie? I've—made all Helen's favorite foods, tonight.

60 [*A pause.*]

61 KELLER [*Gently*]: It's a homecoming party, Miss Annie.

62 [ANNIE *after a moment releases* HELEN. *But she cannot accept it, at her own chair she shakes her head and turns back, intent on* KATE.]

63 ANNIE: She's testing you. You realize?

64 JAMES [*To* ANNIE]: She's testing you.

65 KELLER: Jimmie, be quiet.

66 [JAMES *sits, tense.*]

67 Now she's home, naturally she—

68 ANNIE: And wants to see what will happen. At your hands. I said it was my main worry, is this what you promised me not half an hour ago?

69 KELLER [*Reasonably*]: But she's *not* kicking, now—

70 ANNIE: And not learning not to. Mrs. Keller, teaching her is bound to be painful, to everyone. I know it hurts to watch, but she'll live up to just what you demand of her, and no more.

71 JAMES [*Palely*]: She's testing *you.*

72 KELLER [*Testily*]: Jimmie.

73 JAMES: I have an opinion, I think I should—

74 KELLER: No one's interested in hearing your opinion.

75 ANNIE: *I'm* interested, of course she's testing me. Let me keep her to what she's learned and she'll go on learning from me. Take her out of my hands and it all comes apart.

NOTES

Excerpted from *The Miracle Worker* by William Gibson, published by Scribner.

THINK QUESTIONS

CA-CCSS: CA.RL.7.1, CA.L.7.4a, CA.L.7.4c, CA.L.7.4d

1. Who is Annie Sullivan, and why is she at the Keller homestead in Tuscumbia, Alabama? Cite evidence from information and ideas that are directly stated and from ideas you have inferred from clues in the text.
2. How would you describe Annie's emotions? Why is she feeling this way? Cite evidence from the text to support your answer.
3. What do you think Annie means when she says, "Take her out of my hands and it all comes apart"? Cite evidence from the text to support your answer.
4. Use context clues to determine the meaning of **retrieves** as it is used in the stage directions following Aunt Ev's fifth line of dialogue. Write your definition of *retrieves* and explain how you figured out its meaning. Then confirm your inferred meaning in a print or digital dictionary.
5. Use context clues to figure out the meaning of **indulge** as Captain Keller uses it in his fourth line of dialogue. Write your definition of *indulge* and explain how you figured out the meaning of the word. Find a synonym for *indulge* in a thesaurus and replace it in the sentence to see if it offers the same meaning. Then clarify the precise meaning of *indulge* in a print or digital dictionary.

CLOSE READ

CA-CCSS: CA.RL.7.1, CA.RL.7.2, CA.RL.7.3, CA.W.7.2a, CA.W.7.2b, CA.W.7.2c, CA.W.7.2d, CA.W.7.2e, CA.W.7.2f, CA.W.7.4, CA.W.7.5, CA.W.7.6, CA.W.7.10

Reread the excerpt from the drama "The Miracle Worker." As you reread, complete the Focus Questions below. Then use your answers and annotations from the questions to help you complete the Writing Prompt.

FOCUS QUESTIONS

1. How is the setting important to the dinner scene? What theme can you infer from this setting? Highlight evidence in the dialogue and stage directions to illustrate how the setting affects the theme. Make annotations to record specific textual evidence to support your answer.
2. Highlight a place in the dinner scene where the plot shapes the characters and their interactions with one another. Make annotations to explain your reasoning.
3. Reread the stage directions and dialogue for clues to Annie's character. How do Annie's character traits help shape the plot? Highlight specific textual evidence and make annotations to record your response.
4. Reread the stage directions and the dialogue related to James. What clues do you find about James's character and his role in the plot? Highlight specific textual evidence and make annotations to record your response.
5. The ability of people to transform their lives is one theme in the play. Identify another theme that is related to the challenges of human interactions. Highlight the textual evidence and make annotations to explain the theme.

WRITING PROMPT

How does the interaction of the elements of character, setting, and plot help develop and shape the themes in "The Miracle Worker"? Use the details you have compiled from analyzing the play to identify how

- the setting affects the characters or events of the plot.
- the plot shapes the characters and their relationship to one another.
- the characters influence the plot.
- the dramatic elements help present the theme or themes.

Begin with a clear thesis statement to introduce your topic. Remember to organize and to support your writing with specific evidence and inferences you draw from the text, using precise language and selection vocabulary. Include transitions to show the relationships among your ideas, and use a formal style of writing. Provide a conclusion that summarizes your main ideas.

THE TRAGEDY OF ROMEO AND JULIET

(ACT I, SCENE V)

DRAMA

William Shakespeare

1592

INTRODUCTION

The love story of *Romeo and Juliet* is among Shakespeare's most famous plays. The volatile family feud between the Montagues and Capulets has broken out in violence in the streets of Verona, Italy. With his two friends, Romeo, the son of Lord Montague, attends a party held by Lord Caplulet. A mask hides Romeo's identity. There, he meets and falls in love with the beautiful Juliet, a Capulet. When they first meet, their dialogue comes out as a perfect sonnet, one of three in Shakespeare's tragedy.

"Thus from my lips, by yours, my sin is purged."

FIRST READ

ACT I, SCENE V

A hall in Capulet's house.

1 *Musicians waiting. Enter Servingmen with napkins.*

2 FIRST SERVANT: Where's Potpan, that he helps not to take away? He
3 shift a **trencher**? he scrape a trencher!

4 SECOND SERVANT: When good manners shall lie all in one or two men's
5 hands and they unwashed too, 'tis a foul thing.

6 FIRST SERVANT: Away with the joint-stools, remove the
7 court-cupboard, look to the plate. Good thou, save
8 me a piece of marchpane; and, as thou lovest me, let
9 the porter let in Susan Grindstone and Nell.
10 Antony, and Potpan!

11 SECOND SERVANT: Ay, boy, ready.

12 FIRST SERVANT: You are looked for and called for, asked for and
13 sought for, in the great chamber.

14 SECOND SERVANT: We cannot be here and there too. Cheerly, boys; be
15 brisk awhile, and the longer liver take all.

16 *[Enter CAPULET, with JULIET and others of his house, meeting the Guests and Maskers]*

17 CAPULET: Welcome, gentlemen! ladies that have their toes
18 Unplagued with corns will have a bout with you.

19 Ah ha, my mistresses! which of you all
20 Will now deny to dance? she that makes dainty,
21 She, I'll swear, hath corns; am I come near ye now?
22 Welcome, gentlemen! I have seen the day
23 That I have worn a visor and could tell
24 A whispering tale in a fair lady's ear,
25 Such as would please: 'tis gone, 'tis gone, 'tis gone:
26 You are welcome, gentlemen! come, musicians, play.
27 A hall, a hall! give room! and foot it, girls.
28 *Music plays, and they dance*
29 More light, you knaves; and turn the tables up,
30 And quench the fire, the room is grown too hot.
31 Ah, sirrah, this unlook'd-for sport comes well.
32 Nay, sit, nay, sit, good cousin Capulet;
33 For you and I are past our dancing days:
34 How long is't now since last yourself and I
35 Were in a mask?

36 SECOND CAPULET: By'r lady, thirty years.

37 CAPULET: What, man! 'tis not so much, 'tis not so much:
38 'Tis since the **nuptials** of Lucentio,
39 Come pentecost as quickly as it will,
40 Some five and twenty years; and then we mask'd.

41 SECOND CAPULET: 'Tis more, 'tis more, his son is elder, sir;
42 His son is thirty.

43 CAPULET: Will you tell me that?
44 His son was but a ward two years ago.

45 ROMEO: [*To a Servingman*] What lady is that, which doth
46 enrich the hand
47 Of yonder knight?

48 SERVANT: I know not, sir.

49 ROMEO: O, she doth teach the torches to burn bright!
50 It seems she hangs upon the cheek of night
51 Like a rich jewel in an Ethiope's ear;
52 Beauty too rich for use, for earth too dear!
53 So shows a snowy dove trooping with crows,
54 As yonder lady o'er her fellows shows.
55 The measure done, I'll watch her place of stand,
56 And, touching hers, make blessed my rude hand.
57 Did my heart love till now? forswear it, sight!

NOTES

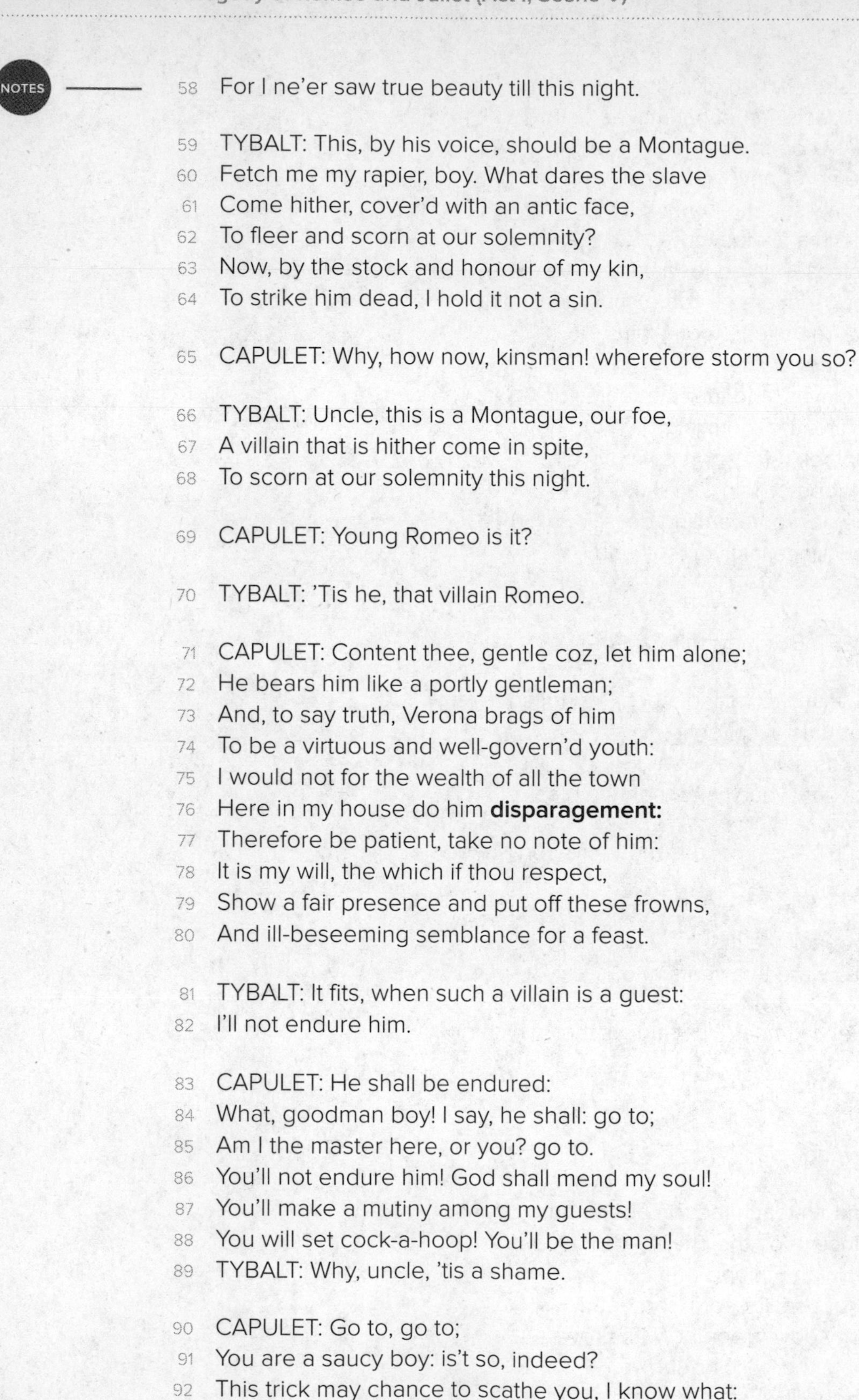

58 For I ne'er saw true beauty till this night.

59 TYBALT: This, by his voice, should be a Montague.
60 Fetch me my rapier, boy. What dares the slave
61 Come hither, cover'd with an antic face,
62 To fleer and scorn at our solemnity?
63 Now, by the stock and honour of my kin,
64 To strike him dead, I hold it not a sin.

65 CAPULET: Why, how now, kinsman! wherefore storm you so?

66 TYBALT: Uncle, this is a Montague, our foe,
67 A villain that is hither come in spite,
68 To scorn at our solemnity this night.

69 CAPULET: Young Romeo is it?

70 TYBALT: 'Tis he, that villain Romeo.

71 CAPULET: Content thee, gentle coz, let him alone;
72 He bears him like a portly gentleman;
73 And, to say truth, Verona brags of him
74 To be a virtuous and well-govern'd youth:
75 I would not for the wealth of all the town
76 Here in my house do him **disparagement:**
77 Therefore be patient, take no note of him:
78 It is my will, the which if thou respect,
79 Show a fair presence and put off these frowns,
80 And ill-beseeming semblance for a feast.

81 TYBALT: It fits, when such a villain is a guest:
82 I'll not endure him.

83 CAPULET: He shall be endured:
84 What, goodman boy! I say, he shall: go to;
85 Am I the master here, or you? go to.
86 You'll not endure him! God shall mend my soul!
87 You'll make a mutiny among my guests!
88 You will set cock-a-hoop! You'll be the man!
89 TYBALT: Why, uncle, 'tis a shame.

90 CAPULET: Go to, go to;
91 You are a saucy boy: is't so, indeed?
92 This trick may chance to scathe you, I know what:
93 You must contrary me! marry, 'tis time.
94 Well said, my hearts! You are a princox; go:

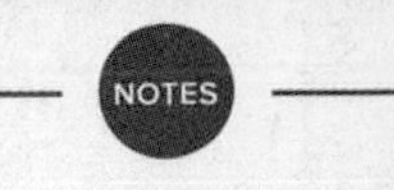

95 Be quiet, or—More light, more light! For shame!
96 I'll make you quiet. What, cheerly, my hearts!

97 TYBALT: Patience perforce with wilful choler meeting
98 Makes my flesh tremble in their different greeting.
99 I will withdraw: but this **intrusion** shall
100 Now seeming sweet convert to bitter gall.

101 *[Exit]*

102 ROMEO [*To JULIET*]: If I **profane** with my unworthiest hand
103 This holy shrine, the gentle fine is this:
104 My lips, two blushing pilgrims, ready stand
105 To smooth that rough touch with a tender kiss.

106 JULIET: Good pilgrim, you do wrong your hand too much,
107 Which mannerly devotion shows in this;
108 For saints have hands that pilgrims' hands do touch,
109 And palm to palm is holy palmers' kiss.

110 ROMEO: Have not saints lips, and holy palmers too?

111 JULIET: Ay, pilgrim, lips that they must use in prayer.

112 ROMEO: O, then, dear saint, let lips do what hands do;
113 They pray, grant thou, lest faith turn to despair.

114 JULIET: Saints do not move, though grant for prayers' sake.

115 ROMEO: Then move not, while my prayer's effect I take.
116 Thus from my lips, by yours, my sin is purged.

117 JULIET: Then have my lips the sin that they have took.

118 ROMEO: Sin from thy lips? O trespass sweetly urged!
119 Give me my sin again.

120 JULIET: You kiss by the book.

121 NURSE: Madam, your mother craves a word with you.

122 ROMEO: What is her mother?

123 NURSE: Marry, bachelor,
124 Her mother is the lady of the house,
125 And a good lady, and a wise and virtuous;
126 I nursed her daughter, that you talk'd withal;

NOTES

127 I tell you, he that can lay hold of her
128 Shall have the chinks.

129 ROMEO: Is she a Capulet?
130 O dear account! my life is my foe's debt.

131 BENVOLIO: Away, begone; the sport is at the best.

132 ROMEO: Ay, so I fear; the more is my unrest.

133 CAPULET: Nay, gentlemen, prepare not to be gone;
134 We have a trifling foolish banquet towards.
135 Is it e'en so? why, then, I thank you all
136 I thank you, honest gentlemen; good night.
137 More torches here! Come on then, let's to bed.
138 Ah, sirrah, by my fay, it waxes late:
139 I'll to my rest.

140 *Exeunt all but JULIET and NURSE*

141 JULIET: Come hither, nurse. What is yond gentleman?

142 NURSE: The son and heir of old Tiberio.

143 JULIET: What's he that now is going out of door?

144 NURSE: Marry, that, I think, be young Petrucio.

145 JULIET: What's he that follows there, that would not dance?

146 NURSE: I know not.

147 JULIET: Go ask his name: if he be married,
148 My grave is like to be my wedding bed.

149 NURSE: His name is Romeo, and a Montague;
150 The only son of your great enemy.

151 JULIET: My only love sprung from my only hate!
152 Too early seen unknown, and known too late!
153 Prodigious birth of love it is to me,
154 That I must love a loathed enemy.

155 NURSE: What's this? What's this?

NOTES

156 JULIET: A rhyme I learn'd even now
157 Of one I danced withal.
158 *[One calls within 'Juliet.']*

159 NURSE: Anon, anon!
160 Come, let's away; the strangers all are gone.

161 *[Exeunt.]*

THINK QUESTIONS CA-CCSS: CA.RL.7.1, CA.L.7.4a, CA.L.7.4b, CA.L.7.4d

1. Refer to two or more details from the text to support your understanding of the setting, why the people are there, and the action that is taking place. Use both direct textual evidence and inferences you can make from the speech and actions of the characters.
2. How do Capulet and Tybalt differ in their reactions to Romeo's crashing the feast as a Masker? Cite specific textual evidence, including lines from the scene's dialogue, and make inferences to support your answer.
3. What evidence is there that Romeo and Juliet experience love at first sight? Cite specific textual evidence from the scene's dialogue to support your answer.
4. By recalling that the Latin suffix *-ment* can mean "the act of," use the context clues provided in Tybalt's and Capulet's angry conversation about Romeo to determine the meaning of *disparagement*. Write your definition of *disparagement* and explain how you determined the meaning of the word.
5. Use context clues to determine the meaning of **profane** as Romeo uses it when speaking to Juliet for the first time. Write your definition of *profane* and explain how you figured out the meaning. Check your inferred meaning in context, or use a print or digital dictionary to verify your definition.

CLOSE READ

CA-CCSS: CA.RL.7.1, CA.RL.7.2, CA.RL.7.4, CA.RL.7.5, CA.W.7.2a, CA.W.7.2b, CA.W.7.2c, CA.W.7.2d, CA.W.7.2e, CA.W.7.2f, CA.W.7.4, CA.W.7.5, CA.W.7.6, CA.W.7.9a, CA.W.7.10, CA.L.7.5a

Reread the excerpt from *The Tragedy of Romeo and Juliet* (Act I, Scene V). As you reread, complete the Focus Questions below. Then use your answers and annotations from the questions to help you complete the Writing Prompt.

FOCUS QUESTIONS

1. Highlight the last two lines in Romeo's second speech and the lines in Tybalt's first speech. How do these lines introduce the reader to the conflict of the plot? Make annotations to explain.

2. What evidence in Tybalt's last speech supports the idea that Tybalt will have a future run-in with Romeo? How does this idea contribute to your understanding of the plot structure of the play? Make annotations to explain your reasoning.

3. What metaphor does Capulet use when he questions Tybalt after Tybalt's first speech? Highlight the metaphor. Make annotations to explain its meaning.

4. In Romeo's second speech, highlight three examples of images that appeal to the sense of sight. (Note that these images may also be part of other figures of speech, such as personification or metaphor.) Make annotations to explain the pictures these images create in the mind of the reader. What do these visual images have in common? What do they reveal about the way Romeo views Juliet?

5. What challenges will Juliet face by falling in love with Romeo? Highlight the textual evidence in Juliet's next-to-last-speech that helps you understand these challenges. Use the annotation tool to show how this evidence relates to the Essential Question of the unit: *What are the challenges of human interactions?* and to the main conflict of the play.

WRITING PROMPT

Think about the rising action of Act I, Scene V in the plot structure of *The Tragedy of Romeo and Juliet*. How does this particular scene contribute to your understanding of the challenges Romeo and Juliet will likely face in their interactions with each other and with other characters? In your response, refer to Shakespeare's use of figurative language in the scene. Begin with a clear thesis statement, and support and organize your response with specific textual evidence. Use transitions to show the relationships among your ideas. Establish a formal style and use precise language and selection vocabulary. Provide an effective conclusion that summarizes your central ideas.

AMIGO BROTHERS

FICTION

Piri Thomas
1978

INTRODUCTION

Piri Thomas grew up in New York City's rough Spanish Harlem neighborhood and began writing his acclaimed autobiography *Down These Mean Streets* while serving a prison term for attempted robbery. Known for the tough reality portrayed in his works, Thomas's literary output includes memoirs, short stories, essays, and poems. In his story "Amigo Brothers," amateur boxers and best friends Antonio and Felix must fight against each other to determine which one will advance to the Golden Gloves Championship.

"Each youngster had a dream of someday becoming lightweight champion of the world."

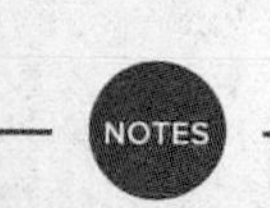

FIRST READ

1 Antonio Cruz and Felix Varga were both seventeen years old. They were so together in friendship that they felt themselves to be brothers. They had known each other since childhood, growing up on the lower east side of Manhattan in the same tenement building on Fifth Street between Avenue A and Avenue B.

2 Antonio was fair, lean, and lanky, while Felix was dark, short, and husky. Antonio's hair was always falling over his eyes, while Felix wore his black hair in a natural Afro style.

3 Each youngster had a dream of someday becoming lightweight champion of the world. Every chance they had the boys worked out, sometimes at the Boys Club on 10th Street and Avenue A and sometimes at the pro's gym on 14th Street. Early morning sunrises would find them running along the East River Drive, wrapped in sweat shirts, short towels around their necks, and handkerchiefs Apache style around their foreheads.

4 While some youngsters were into street negatives, Antonio and Felix slept, ate, rapped, and dreamt positive. Between them, they had a collection of second to none, plus a scrapbook filled with torn tickets to every boxing match they had ever attended, and some clippings of their own. If asked a question about any given fighter, they would immediately zip out from their memory banks divisions, weights, records of fights, knock-outs, technical knock-outs, and draws or losses.

5 Each had fought many **bouts** representing their community and had won two gold-plated medals plus a silver and bronze medallion. The difference was in their style. Antonio's lean form and long reach made him the better boxer, while Felix's short and muscular frame made him the better slugger. Whenever

they had met in the ring for sparring sessions, it had always been hot and heavy.

6 Now, after a series of elimination bouts, they had been informed that they were to meet each other in the division finals that were scheduled for the seventh of August, two weeks away—the winner to represent the Boys Club in the Golden Gloves Championship Tournament.

7 The two boys continued to run together along the East River Drive. But even when joking with each other, they both sensed a wall rising between them.

8 One morning less than a week before their bout, they met as usual for their daily work-out. They fooled around with a few jabs at the air, slapped skin, and then took off, running lightly along the dirty East River's edge.

9 Antonio glanced at Felix who kept his eyes purposely straight ahead, pausing from time to time to do some fancy leg work while throwing one-twos followed by upper cuts to an imaginary jaw. Antonio then beat the air with a **barrage** of body blows and short devastating lefts with an overhand jaw-breaking right.

10 After a mile or so, Felix puffed and said, "Let's stop a while, bro. I think we both got something to say to each other."

11 Antonio nodded. It was not natural to be acting as though nothing unusual was happening when two aceboon buddies were going to be blasting each other within a few short days.

12 They rested their elbows on the railing separating them from the river. Antonio wiped his face with his short towel. The sunrise was now creating day.

13 Felix leaned heavily on the river's railing and stared across to the shores of Brooklyn. Finally, he broke the silence.

14 "Man, I don't know how to come out with it."

15 Antonio helped. "It's about our fight, right?"

16 "Yeah, right." Felix's eyes squinted at the rising orange sun.

17 "I've been thinking about it too, *panin*. In fact, since we found out it was going to be me and you, I've been awake at night, pulling punches on you, trying not to hurt you."

18 "Same here. It ain't natural not to think about the fight. I mean, we both are *cheverote* fighters and we both want to win. But only one of us can win. There ain't no draws in the eliminations."

19 Felix tapped Antonio gently on the shoulder. "I don't mean to sound like I'm bragging, bro. But I wanna win, fair and square."

20 Antonio nodded quietly. "Yeah. We both know that in the ring the better man wins. Friend or no friend, brother or no. . ."

21 Felix finished it for him. "Brother. Tony, let's promise something right here. Okay?"

22 "If it's fair, *hermano,* I'm for it." Antonio admired the courage of a tug boat pulling a barge five times its welterweight size.

23 "It's fair, Tony. When we get into the ring, it's gotta be like we never met. We gotta be like two heavy strangers that want the same thing and only one can have it. You understand, don'tcha?"

24 "*Si,* I know." Tony smiled. "No pulling punches. We go all the way."

25 "Yeah, that's right. Listen, Tony. Don't you think it's a good idea if we don't see each other until the day of the fight? I'm going to stay with my Aunt Lucy in the Bronx. I can use Gleason's Gym for working out. My manager says he got some sparring partners with more or less your style."

26 Tony scratched his nose **pensively**. "Yeah, it would be better for our heads." He held out his hand, palm upward. "Deal?"

27 "Deal." Felix lightly slapped open skin.

28 "Ready for some more running?" Tony asked lamely.

29 "Naw, bro. Let's cut it here. You go on. I kinda like to get things together in my head."

30 "You ain't worried, are you?" Tony asked.

31 "No way, man." Felix laughed out loud. "I got too much smarts for that. I just think it's cooler if we split right here. After the fight, we can get it together again like nothing ever happened."

32 The amigo brothers were not ashamed to hug each other tightly.

33 "Guess you're right. Watch yourself, Felix. I hear there's some pretty heavy dudes up in the Bronx. *Suavecito,* okay?"

34 "Okay. You watch yourself too, *sabe?*"

NOTES

35 Tony jogged away. Felix watched his friend disappear from view, throwing rights and lefts. Both fighters had a lot of psyching up to do before the big fight.

36 The days in training passed much too slowly. Although they kept out of each other's way, they were aware of each other's progress via the ghetto grapevine.

37 The evening before the big fight, Tony made his way to the roof of his tenement. In the quiet early dark, he peered over the ledge. Six stories below the lights of the city blinked and the sounds of cars mingled with the curses and the laughter of children in the street. He tried not to think of Felix, feeling he had succeeded in psyching his mind. But only in the ring would he really know. To spare Felix hurt, he would have to knock him out, early and quick.

38 Up in the South Bronx, Felix decided to take in a movie in an effort to keep Antonio's face away from his fists. The flick was *The Champion* with Kirk Douglas, the third time Felix was seeing it.

39 The champion was getting the daylights beat out of him. He was saved only by the sound of the bell.

40 Felix became the champ and Tony the challenger.

41 The movie audience was going out of its head. The champ hunched his shoulders grunting and sniffing red blood back into his broken nose. The challenger, confident that he had the championship in the bag, threw a left. The champ countered with a dynamite right.

42 Felix's right arm felt the shock, Antonio's face, superimposed on the screen, was hit by the awesome force of the blow. Felix saw himself in the ring, blasting Antonio against the ropes. The champ had to be forcibly restrained. The challenger fell slowly to the canvas.

43 When Felix finally left the theatre, he had figured out how to psyche himself for tomorrow's fight. It was Felix the Champion vs. Antonio the Challenger.

44 He walked up some dark streets, deserted except for small pockets of wary-looking kids wearing gang colors.

45 Despite the fact that he was Puerto Rican like them, they eyed him as a stranger to their turf. Felix did a fast shuffle, bobbing and weaving, while letting loose a torrent of blows that would demolish whatever got in its way. It seemed to impress the brothers, who went about their own business.

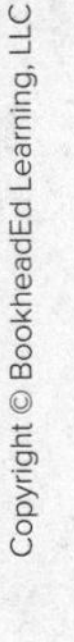

46 Finding no takers, Felix decided to split to his aunt's. Walking the streets had not relaxed him, neither had the fight flick. All it had done was to stir him up. He let himself quietly into his Aunt Lucy's apartment and went straight to bed, falling into a fitful sleep with sounds of the gong for Round One.

47 Antonio was passing some heavy time on his rooftop. How would the fight tomorrow affect his relationship with Felix? After all, fighting was like any other profession. Friendship had nothing to do with it. A gnawing doubt crept in. He cut negative thinking real quick by doing some speedy fancy dance steps, bobbing and weaving like mercury. The night air was blurred with perpetual motions of left hooks and right crosses. Felix, his *amigo* brother, was not going to be Felix at all in the ring. Just an opponent with another face. Antonio went to sleep, hearing the opening bell for the first round. Like his friend in the South Bronx, he prayed for victory, via a quick clean knock-out in the first round.

48 Large posters plastered all over the walls of local shops announced the fight between Antonio Cruz and Felix Vargas as the main bout.

49 The fight had created great interest in the neighborhood. Antonio and Felix were well liked and respected. Each had his own loyal following.

50 Antonio's fans had unbridled faith in his boxing skills. On the other side, Felix's admirers trusted in his dynamite-packed fists.

51 Felix had returned to his apartment early in the morning of August 7th and stayed there, hoping to avoid seeing Antonio. He turned the radio on to *salsa* music sounds and then tried to read while waiting for word from his manager.

52 The fight was scheduled to take place in Tompkins Square Park. It had been decided that the gymnasium of the Boys Club was not large enough to hold all the people who were sure to attend. In Tompkins Square Park, everyone who wanted could view the fight, whether from ringside or window fire escapes or tenement rooftops.

53 The morning of the fight Tompkins Square was a beehive of activity with numerous workers setting up the ring, the seats, and the guest speakers' stand. The scheduled bouts began shortly after noon and the park had begun filling up even earlier.

54 The local junior high school across from Tompkins Square Park served as the dressing room for all the fighters. Each was given a separate classroom with desk tops, covered with mats, serving as resting tables. Antonio thought he caught a glimpse of Felix waving to him from a room at the end of the corridor. He waved back just in case it had been him.

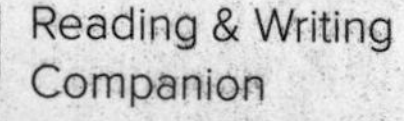

NOTES

55 The fighters changed from their street clothes into fighting gear. Antonio wore white trunks, black socks, and black shoes. Felix wore sky blue trunks, red socks, and white boxing shoes. Each had dressing gowns to match their fighting trunks with their names neatly stitched on the back.

56 The loudspeakers blared into the open windows of the school. There were speeches by dignitaries, community leaders, and great boxers of yesteryear. Some were well prepared, some improvised on the spot. They all carried the same message of great pleasure and honor at being part of such a historic event. This great day was in the tradition of champions emerging from the streets of the lower east side.

57 Interwoven with the speeches were the sounds of the other boxing events. After the sixth bout, Felix was much relieved when his trainer Charlie said, "Time change. Quick knock-out. This is it. We're on."

58 Waiting time was over. Felix was escorted from the classroom by a dozen fans in white T-shirts with the word FELIX across their fronts.

59 Antonio was escorted down a different stairwell and guided through a roped-off path.

60 As the two climbed into the ring, the crowd exploded with a roar. Antonio and Felix both bowed gracefully and then raised their arms in acknowledgment.

61 Antonio tried to be cool, but even as the roar was in its first birth, he turned slowly to meet Felix's eyes looking directly into his. Felix nodded his head and Antonio responded. And both as one, just as quickly, turned away to face his own corner.

62 Bong—bong—bong. The roar turned to stillness.

63 "Ladies and Gentlemen, *Señores y Señoras*."

64 The announcer spoke slowly, pleased at his bilingual efforts.

65 "Now the moment we have all been waiting for—the main event between two fine young Puerto Rican fighters, products of our lower east side.

66 "In this corner, weighing 134 pounds, Felix Vargas. And in this corner, weighing 133 pounds, Antonio Cruz. The winner will represent the Boys Club in the tournament of champions, the Golden Gloves. There will be no draw. May the best man win."

67 The cheering of the crowd shook the window panes of the old buildings surrounding Tompkins Square Park. At the center of the ring, the referee was giving instructions to the youngsters.

NOTES

68 "Keep your punches up. No low blows. No punching on the back of the head. Keep your heads up. Understand. Let's have a clean fight. Now shake hands and come out fighting."

69 Both youngsters touched gloves and nodded. They turned and danced quickly to their corners . Their head towels and dressing gowns were lifted neatly from their shoulders by their trainers' nimble fingers. Antonio crossed himself. Felix did the same.

70 BONG! BONG! ROUND ONE. Felix and Antonio turned and faced each other squarely in a fighting pose. Felix wasted no time. He came in fast, head low, half hunched toward his right shoulder, and lashed out with a straight left. He missed a right cross as Antonio slipped the punch and countered with one-two-three lefts that snapped Felix's head back, sending a mild shock coursing through him. If Felix had any small doubt about their friendship affecting their fight, it was being neatly **dispelled**.

71 Antonio danced, a joy to behold. His left hand was like a piston pumping jabs one right after another with seeming ease. Felix bobbed and weaved and never stopped boring in. He knew that at long range he was at a disadvantage. Antonio had too much reach on him. Only by coming in close could Felix hope to achieve the dreamed-of knockout.

72 Antonio knew the dynamite that was stored in his *amigo* brother's fist. He ducked a short right and missed a left hook. Felix trapped him against the ropes just long enough to pour some punishing rights and lefts to Antonio's hard midsection. Antonio slipped away from Felix, crashing two lefts to his head, which set Felix's right ear to ringing.

73 Bong! Both *amigos* froze a punch well on its way, sending up a roar of approval for good sportsmanship.

74 Felix walked briskly back to his corner. His right ear had not stopped ringing. Antonio gracefully danced his way toward his stool none the worse, except for glowing glove burns, showing angry red against the whiteness of his midribs.

75 "Watch that right, Tony." His trainer talked into his ear. "Remember Felix always goes to the body. He'll want you to drop your hands for his overhand left or right. Got it?"

76 Antonio nodded, spraying water out between his teeth. He felt better as his sore midsection was being firmly rubbed.

77 Felix's corner was also busy.

NOTES

78 "You gotta get in there, fella." Felix's trainer poured water over his curly Afro locks. "Get in there or he's gonna chop you up from way back."

79 *Bong! Bong!* Round two. Felix was off his stool and rushed Antonio like a bull, sending a hard right to his head. Beads of water exploded from Antonio's long hair.

80 Antonio, hurt, sent back a blurring barrage of lefts and rights that only meant pain to Felix, who returned with a short left to the head followed by a looping right to the body. Antonio countered with his own flurry, forcing Felix to give ground. But not for long.

81 Felix bobbed and weaved, bobbed and weaved, occasionally punching his two gloves together.

82 Antonio waited for the rush that was sure to come. Felix closed in and feinted with his left shoulder and threw his right instead. Lights suddenly exploded inside Felix's head as Antonio slipped the blow and hit him with a pistonlike left, catching him flush on the point of his chin.

83 Badlam broke loose as Felix's legs momentarily buckled. He fought off a series of rights and lefts and came back with a strong right that taught Antonio respect.

84 Antonio danced in carefully. He knew Felix had the habit of playing possum when hurt, to sucker an opponent within reach of the powerful bombs he carried in each fist.

85 A right to the head slowed Antonio's pretty dancing. He answered with his own left at Felix's right eye that began puffing up within three seconds.

86 Antonio, a bit too eager, moved in too close and Felix had him entangled into a rip-roaring, punching toe-to-toe slugfest that brought the whole Tompkins Square Park screaming to its feet.

87 Rights to the body. Lefts to the head. Neither fighter was giving an inch. Suddenly a short right caught Antonio squarely on the chin. His long legs turned to jelly and his arms flailed out desperately. Felix, grunting like a bull, threw wild punches from every direction. Antonio, groggy, bobbed and weaved, evading most of the blows. Suddenly his head cleared. His left flashed out hard and straight catching Felix on the bridge of his nose.

88 Felix lashed back with a haymaker, right off the ghetto streets. At the same instant, his eye caught another left hook from Antonio. Felix swung out trying to clear the pain. Only the **frenzied** screaming of those along the ringside let him know that he had dropped Antonio. Fighting off the growing haze,

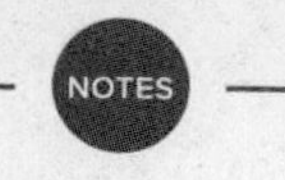

Antonio struggled to his feet, got up, ducked, and threw a smashing right that dropped Felix flat on his back.

89 Felix got up as fast as he could in his own corner, groggy but still game. He didn't even hear the count. In a fog, he heard the roaring of the crowd, who seemed to have gone insane. His head cleared to hear the bell sound at the end of the round. He was very glad. His trainer sat his down on the stool.

90 In his corner, Antonio was doing what all fighters do when they are hurt. They sit and smile at everyone.

91 The referee signaled the ring doctor to check the fighters outs. He did so and then gave his okay. The cold water sponges brought clarity to both *amigo* brothers. They were rubbed until their circulation ran free.

92 *Bong!* Round three—the final round. Up to now it had been tic-tac-toe, pretty much even. But everyone knew there could be no draw and that this round would decide the winner.

93 This time, to Felix's surprise, it was Antonio who came out fast, charging across the ring. Felix braced himself but couldn't ward off the barrage of punches. Antonio drove Felix hard against the ropes.

94 The crowd ate it up. Thus far the two had fought with *mucho corazón*. Felix tapped his gloves and commenced his attack anew. Antonio, throwing boxer's caution to the winds, jumped in to meet him.

95 Both pounded away. Neither gave an inch and neither fell to the canvas. Felix's left eye was tightly closed. Claret red blood poured from Antonio's nose. They fought toe-to-toe.

96 The sounds of their blows were loud in contrast to the silence of a crowd gone completely mute.

97 *Bong! Bong! Bong!* The bell sounded over and over again. Felix and Antonio were past hearing. Their blows continued to pound on each other like hailstones.

98 Finally the referee and the two trainers pried Felix and Antonio apart. Cold water was poured over them to bring them back to their senses.

99 They looked around and then rushed toward each other. A cry of alarm surged through Tompkins Square Park. Was this a fight to the death instead of a boxing match?

NOTES

100 The fear soon gave way to wave upon wave of cheering as the two *amigos* embraced.

101 No matter what the decision, they knew they would always be champions to each other.

102 *BONG! BONG! BONG!* "Ladies and Gentlemen. *Señores* and *Señoras*. The winner and representative to the Golden Gloves Tournament of Champions is. . ."

103 The announcer turned to point to the winner and found himself alone. Arm in arm the champions had already left the ring.

THINK QUESTIONS

CA-CCSS: CA.RL.7.1, CA.L.7.4a, CA.L.7.4b, CA.L.7.4c, CA.L.7.4d

1. Why does the author refer to Antonio Cruz and Feliz Varga as the "amigo brothers"? How were the boys alike? How were they different? Cite specific evidence from paragraphs 1–3 to support your answer.
2. How does the reader know that boxing was very important to Antonio and Felix? Cite specific evidence from paragraphs 3 and 4 to support your response.
3. Why was the upcoming division match a challenge for Antonio and Felix's friendship? How did the boys have the same point of view about handling the match? Cite specific evidence from paragraphs 11–25 to support your response.
4. Use context clues to determine the meaning of the word **dispelled** as it is used at the beginning of the fight scene, in paragraph 70 of "Amigo Brothers." Write your definition of *dispelled,* and explain how you figured out the meaning of the word. Then check your meaning in a print or digital dictionary.
5. Use context clues and word origin to figure out the meaning of **frenzied** as it is used during the heat of the fight, in paragraph 88 of "Amigo Brothers." Write your definition of *frenzied* and tell how you determined the meaning of the word. Consult a print or digital dictionary to find the interesting word origin (or etymology) of *frenzied* that will help you figure out its meaning. Then check the dictionary again to clarify the precise meaning of the word.

CLOSE READ

CA-CCSS: CA.RL.7.1, CA.RL.7.2, CA.RL.7.3, CA.RL.7.6, CA.W.7.2a, CA.W.7.2b, CA.W.7.2c, CA.W.7.2d, CA.W.7.2e, CA.W.7.2f, CA.W.7.4, CA.W.7.5, CA.W.7.6, CA.W.7.9a, CA.W.7.10

Reread the story "Amigo Brothers." As you reread, complete the Focus Questions below. Then use your answers and annotations from the questions to help you complete the Writing Prompt.

FOCUS QUESTIONS

1. As you reread "Amigo Brothers," keep in mind that the story is told from the third-person point of view. Although readers can infer much about the boys' character traits and point of view from their dialogue, the narrator also provides important information about the boys. Highlight evidence in paragraph 4 that reveals how the narrator feels about Antonio and Felix. How does this information help you determine the theme? Make annotations to explain your ideas.

2. Dialogue can also reveal character traits and point of view, thereby helping to uncover the theme, or underlying message, of a text. What point of view do Antonio and Felix share in paragraphs 23–27? How does their shared point of view help you discover the theme? Highlight textual evidence and make annotations to explain your thinking.

3. What evidence is there in paragraphs 37–38 and 47 that Antonio and Felix are conflicted about the fight? How does this conflict relate to the theme? Highlight textual evidence and make annotations to explain your response.

4. Which lines from paragraph 54 provide strong evidence of the theme of the story? Highlight the two most important sentences and annotate how they express the theme.

5. How does the theme of the story teach a lesson about the challenges of human interactions? Highlight textual evidence and make annotations to support your answer.

WRITING PROMPT

How does the theme of "Amigo Brothers" help you understand a larger lesson about life, human nature, or human experience? Use the details and evidence you have compiled from examining the story elements of setting, character and dialogue, conflict and plot, and point of view to

- identify the theme of the story.
- analyze how the theme (or underlying message) is developed over the course of the text.

Begin with a clear thesis statement that introduces your topic. Remember to organize and support your writing with textual evidence and inferences, using precise language and selection vocabulary where possible. Include transitions to reveal the connections among your ideas, and establish a formal style of delivery. Finally, provide a conclusion that summarizes your main ideas.

THANK YOU, M'AM

FICTION

Langston Hughes

1958

INTRODUCTION

Langston Hughes was working as a busboy in Washington, D.C. when he showed some of his poems to famous poet Vachel Lindsay. Lindsay was so impressed that he read the poems that night to an audience. In time, Hughes became one of the first African Americans to make a living as a writer and lecturer, eventually moving back to New York and becoming a leader of the Harlem Renaissance. In Hughes's short story "Thank You, M'am," a teenage boy tries to snatch a woman's purse late one night and is surprised by what happens next.

"'You gonna take me to jail?' asked the boy..."

FIRST READ

Excerpt from Chapter 2: All Was Not Right

1 She was a large woman with a large purse that had everything in it but hammer and nails. It had a long strap, and she carried it slung across her shoulder. It was about eleven o'clock at night, and she was walking alone, when a boy ran up behind her and tried to snatch her purse. The strap broke with the single tug the boy gave it from behind. But the boy's weight and the weight of the purse combined caused him to lose his balance so, instead of taking off full blast as he had hoped, the boy fell on his back on the sidewalk, and his legs flew up. The large woman simply turned around and kicked him right square in his blue-jeaned sitter. Then she reached down, picked the boy up by his shirt front, and shook him until his teeth rattled.

2 After that the woman said, "Pick up my pocketbook, boy, and give it here." She still held him. But she bent down enough to permit him to stoop and pick up her purse. Then she said, "Now ain't you ashamed of yourself?"

3 Firmly gripped by his shirt front, the boy said, "Yes'm."

4 The woman said, "What did you want to do it for?"

5 The boy said, "I didn't aim to."

6 She said, "You a lie!"

7 By that time two or three people passed, stopped, turned to look, and some stood watching.

8 "If I turn you loose, will you run?" asked the woman.

9 "Yes'm," said the boy.

NOTES

10 "Then I won't turn you loose," said the woman. She did not release him.

11 "I'm very sorry, lady, I'm sorry," whispered the boy.

12 "Um-hum! And your face is dirty. I got a great mind to wash your face for you. Ain't you got nobody home to tell you to wash your face?"

13 "No'm," said the boy.

14 "Then it will get washed this evening," said the large woman starting up the street, dragging the frightened boy behind her.

15 He looked as if he were fourteen or fifteen, **frail** and willow-wild, in tennis shoes and blue jeans.

16 The woman said, "You ought to be my son. I would teach you right from wrong. Least I can do right now is to wash your face. Are you hungry?"

17 "No'm," said the being dragged boy. "I just want you to turn me loose."

18 "Was I bothering *you* when I turned that corner?" asked the woman.

19 "No'm."

20 "But you put yourself in contact with *me,*" said the woman. "If you think that that contact is not going to last awhile, you got another thought coming. When I get through with you, sir, you are going to remember Mrs. Luella Bates Washington Jones."

21 Sweat popped out on the boy's face and he began to struggle. Mrs. Jones stopped, jerked him around in front of her, put a half-nelson about his neck, and continued to drag him up the street. When she got to her door, she dragged the boy inside, down a hall, and into a large kitchenette furnished room at the rear of the house. She switched on the light and left the door open. The boy could hear other **roomers** laughing and talking in the large house. Some of their doors were open, too, so he knew he and the woman were not alone. The woman still had him by the neck in the middle of her room.

22 She said, "What is your name?"

23 "Roger," answered the boy.

24 "Then, Roger, you go to that sink and wash your face," said the woman, whereupon she turned him loose—at last. Roger looked at the door—looked at the woman—looked at the door—*and went to the sink.*

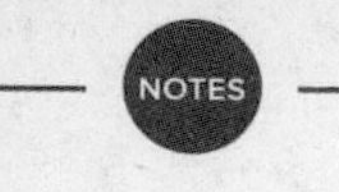

25 "Let the water run until it gets warm," she said. "Here's a clean towel."

26 "You gonna take me to jail?" asked the boy, bending over the sink.

27 "Not with that face, I would not take you nowhere," said the woman. "Here I am trying to get home to cook me a bite to eat and you snatch my pocketbook! Maybe, you ain't been to your supper either, late as it be. Have you?"

28 "There's nobody home at my house," said the boy.

29 "Then we'll eat," said the woman, "I believe you're hungry—or been hungry—to try to snatch my pocketbook."

30 "I wanted a pair of blue suede shoes," said the boy.

31 "Well, you didn't have to snatch *my* pocketbook to get some suede shoes," said Mrs. Luella Bates Washington Jones. "You could of asked me."

32 "M'am?"

33 The water dripping from his face, the boy looked at her. There was a long pause. A very long pause. After he had dried his face and not knowing what else to do dried it again, the boy turned around, wondering what next. The door was open. He could make a dash for it down the hall. He could run, run, run, run, *run!*

34 The woman was sitting on the **day-bed**. After a while she said, "I were young once and I wanted things I could not get."

35 There was another long pause. The boy's mouth opened. Then he frowned, but not knowing he frowned.

36 The woman said, "Um-hum! You thought I was going to say but, didn't you? You thought I was going to say, *but I didn't snatch people's pocketbooks*. Well, I wasn't going to say that." Pause. Silence. "I have done things, too, which I would not tell you, son—neither tell God, if he didn't already know. So you set down while I fix us something to eat. You might run that comb through your hair so you will look **presentable**."

37 In another corner of the room behind a screen was a gas plate and an icebox. Mrs. Jones got up and went behind the screen. The woman did not watch the boy to see if he was going to run now, nor did she watch her purse which she left behind her on the day-bed. But the boy took care to sit on the far side of the room where he thought she could easily see him out of the corner of her eye, if she wanted to. He did not trust the woman *not* to trust him. And he did not want to be **mistrusted** now.

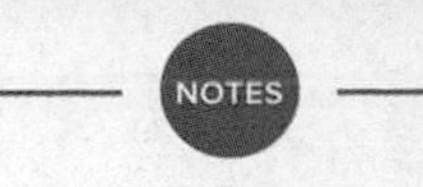

38 "Do you need somebody to go to the store," asked the boy, "maybe to get some milk or something?"

39 "Don't believe I do," said the woman, "unless you just want sweet milk yourself. I was going to make cocoa out of this canned milk I got here."

40 "That will be fine," said the boy.

41 She heated some lima beans and ham she had in the icebox, made the cocoa, and set the table. The woman did not ask the boy anything about where he lived, or his folks, or anything else that would embarrass him. Instead, as they ate, she told him about her job in a hotel beauty-shop that stayed open late, what the work was like, and how all kinds of women came in and out, blondes, red-heads, and Spanish. Then she cut him a half of her ten-cent cake.

42 "Eat some more, son," she said.

43 When they were finished eating she got up and said, "Now, here, take this ten dollars and buy yourself some blue suede shoes. And next time, do not make the mistake of latching onto *my* pocketbook *nor nobody else's*—because shoes come by devilish like that will burn your feet. I got to get my rest now. But I wish you would behave yourself, son, from here on in."

44 She led him down the hall to the front door and opened it. "Good-night! Behave yourself, boy!" she said, looking out into the street.

45 The boy wanted to say something else other than "Thank you, m'am" to Mrs. Luella Bates Washington Jones, but he couldn't do so as he turned at the barren stoop and looked back at the large woman in the door. He barely managed to say "Thank you" before she shut the door. And he never saw her again.

THINK QUESTIONS CA-CCSS: CA.RL.7.1, CA.L.7.4a, CA.L.7.4b, CA.L.7.4d

1. What event brought Roger and Mrs. Luella Bates Washington Jones into contact? What was Mrs. Jones's immediate reaction to this event? Cite specific evidence from the text to support your response.

2. Rather than call the police, what does Mrs. Jones do to Roger? How does Roger initially respond? Cite specific evidence from the text to support your analysis.

3. What does Roger say when Mrs. Jones asks him why he tried to snatch her pocketbook? What does Mrs. Jones say in response? How do her words affect him? Cite specific evidence from the text to support your statements.

4. By recalling that the suffix *-er* means "a person who lives in," use the base word *room* and the suffix *-er* to determine the meaning of **roomers**. Then use context clues to confirm the meaning of the word as it is used in paragraph 21 of "Thank You, M'am." Write your definition of *roomers* and explain how you figured out the word's meaning.

5. Use the context clues provided in paragraph 37 to determine the meaning of **mistrusted**. Write your definition of *mistrusted* and verify your meaning of the word in a print or digital dictionary.

CLOSE READ

CA-CCSS: CA.RL.7.1, CA.RL.7.2, CA.RL.7.3, CA.W.7.2a, CA.W.7.2b, CA.W.7.2c, CA.W.7.2d, CA.W.7.2e, CA.W.7.2f

Reread the short story "Thank You, M'am." Then use your answers and annotations from the questions to help you complete the Writing Prompt.

FOCUS QUESTIONS

1. What evidence is there in paragraphs 1 and 2 that Mrs. Jones is feeling no empathy or kindness toward Roger when they first meet? Highlight the evidence in the text and make annotations to explain your choices.
2. Reread paragraphs 21–25. What emotional changes take place between Mrs. Jones and Roger over the course of these five paragraphs? Highlight the textual evidence. Make annotations to explain the significance of these changes for Mrs. Jones and Roger.
3. In paragraph 41, what does Mrs. Jones avoid asking Roger? Why do you think she does this? What does this tell you about her relationship with him at this point in the story? Highlight textual evidence and make annotations to explain your ideas.
4. Highlight the lines in paragraph 43 that may provide evidence of the story's theme. Then make annotations to explain how the evidence may suggest the possible message, or theme.
5. How do Mrs. Jones and Roger interact with each other at the beginning of the story? How does their interaction change as the story progresses? How do these changes enable the characters to overcome the challenges of their first interaction? Highlight textual evidence and make annotations to support your response.

WRITING PROMPT

How does the setting of "Thank You, M'am" shape the plot and the characters of the story? How do the setting, characters, and plot contribute to your understanding of the theme? Begin with a clear thesis statement. Use the details you have compiled from examining the story elements of setting, plot, and characters to

- explain how the setting helps shape the characters and plot.
- identify how the characters change over the course of the text.
- identify the theme (or message) of the story.

Remember to organize and to support your writing with evidence and inferences drawn from the text. Use precise language and selection vocabulary to support your inferences. Establish and maintain a formal writing style, and include transitions to show connections among your ideas. Provide a conclusion that summarizes your key points and leaves your readers with something to think about.

CALIFORNIA INVASIVE PLANT INVENTORY

NON-FICTION

California Invasive Plant Council
2006

INTRODUCTION

studysync tv

Invasive species are plants, animals, or other organisms that are introduced to an area outside their original range, often by human activity, and cause harm in the new habitat by displacing native species and altering the environment. In California, there are more than 200 invasive plant species alone, ranging from Australia's silver wattle to Japanese eelgrass to the giant reed, a tall cane native to India that is choking waterways throughout the southwestern United States. As described here, the California Invasive Plant Council maintains a detailed inventory of invasive species to help track the threat and control the spread of intruders.

"Approximately 1,800 non-native plants also grow in the wild in the state."

FIRST READ

NOTES

Excerpt from Chapter 15

1 The California **Invasive** Plant **Inventory categorizes** non-native invasive plants that threaten the state's wildlands. Categorization is based on an assessment of the **ecological impacts** of each plant. The Inventory represents the best available knowledge of invasive plant experts in the state. However, it has no regulatory authority, and should be used with full understanding of the limitations described below.

2 California is home to 4,200 native plant species, and is recognized internationally as a "biodiversity hotspot." Approximately 1,800 non-native plants also grow in the wild in the state. A small number of these, approximately 200, are the ones that this Inventory considers invasive. Improved understanding of their impacts will help those working to protect California's treasured biodiversity.

The Inventory

3 The Inventory categorizes plants as High, Moderate, or Limited, reflecting the level of each species' negative ecological impact in California. Other factors, such as economic impact or difficulty of management, are not included in this assessment. It is important to note that even Limited species are invasive and should be of concern to land managers. Although the impact of each plant varies regionally, its rating represents cumulative impacts statewide. Therefore, a plant whose statewide impacts are categorized as Limited may have more severe impacts in a particular region. Conversely, a plant categorized as having a High cumulative impact across California may have very little impact in some regions.

4 The Inventory Review Committee, Cal-IPC staff, and volunteers drafted assessments for each plant based on the formal **criteria** system described below. The committee solicited information from land managers across the

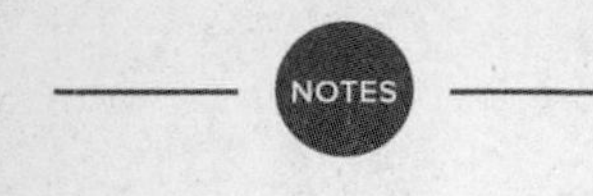

state to complement the available literature. Assessments were released for public review before the committee finalized them. The 2006 list includes 39 High species, 65 Moderate species, and 89 Limited species. Additional information, including updated observations, will be added to this website periodically, with revisions tracked and dated.

Definitions

5 The Inventory categorizes "invasive non-native plants that threaten wildlands" according to the definitions below. Plants were evaluated only if they invade California wildlands with native habitat values. The Inventory does not include plants found solely in areas of human-caused disturbance such as roadsides and cultivated agricultural fields.

6 *Wildlands* are public and private lands that support native **ecosystems,** including some working landscapes such as grazed rangeland and active timberland.

7 *Non-native plants* are species introduced to California after European contact and as a direct or indirect result of human activity.

8 *Invasive non-native plants that threaten wildlands* are plants that 1) are not native to, yet can spread into, wildland ecosystems, and that also 2) displace native species, hybridize with native species, alter biological communities, or alter ecosystem processes.

Criteria for Listing

9 The California Invasive Plant Inventory updates the 1999 "Exotic Pest Plants of Greatest Ecological Concern in California." Cal-IPC's Inventory Review Committee met regularly between 2002 and 2005 to review 238 non-native species with known or suspected impacts in California wildlands. These assessments are based on the "Criteria for Categorizing Invasive Non-Native Plants that Threaten Wildlands," developed in collaboration with the Southwestern Vegetation Management Association in Arizona and the University of Nevada Cooperative Extension so that ratings could be applied across political boundaries and adjusted for regional variation.

10 The goals of the criteria system and the Inventory are to: Provide a uniform methodology for categorizing non-native invasive plants that threaten wildlands; Provide a clear explanation of the process used to evaluate and categorize plants; Provide flexibility so the criteria can be adapted to the particular needs of different regions and states; Encourage contributions of data and documentation on evaluated species; Educate policy makers, land managers, and the public about the biology, ecological impacts, and distribution of invasive non-native plants.

NOTES

11 The criteria system generates a plant's overall rating based on an evaluation of 13 criteria, which are divided into three sections assessing Ecological Impacts, Invasive Potential, and Ecological Distribution. Evaluators assign a score of A (severe) to D (no impact) for each criterion, with U indicating unknown. The scoring scheme is arranged in a tiered format, with individual criteria contributing to section scores that in turn generate an overall rating for the plant. Detailed plant assessment forms list the rationale and applicable references used to arrive at each criterion's score. The level of documentation for each question is also rated, and translated into a numerical score for averaging. The documentation score presented in the tables is a numeric average of the documentation levels for all 13 criteria.

Inventory Categories

12 Each plant on the list received an overall rating of High, Moderate, or Limited based on evaluation using the criteria system. The meaning of these overall ratings is described below. In addition to the overall ratings, specific combinations of section scores that indicate significant potential for invading new ecosystems triggers an Alert designation so that land managers may watch for range expansions. Some plants were categorized as Evaluated But Not Listed because either we lack sufficient information to assign a rating or the available information indicates that the species does not have significant impacts at the present time.

13 High – These species have severe ecological impacts on physical processes, plant and animal communities, and vegetation structure. Their reproductive biology and other attributes are conducive to moderate to high rates of dispersal and establishment. Most are widely distributed ecologically.

14 Moderate – These species have substantial and apparent—but generally not severe—ecological impacts on physical processes, plant and animal communities, and vegetation structure. Their reproductive biology and other attributes are conducive to moderate to high rates of dispersal, though establishment is generally dependent upon ecological disturbance. Ecological amplitude and distribution may range from limited to widespread.

15 Limited – These species are invasive but their ecological impacts are minor on a statewide level or there was not enough information to justify a higher score. Their reproductive biology and other attributes result in low to moderate rates of invasiveness. Ecological amplitude and distribution are generally limited, but these species may be locally persistent and problematic.

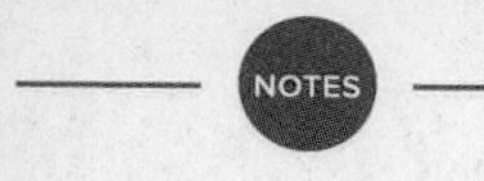

Uses and Limitations

16 The California Invasive Plant Inventory serves as a scientific and educational report. It is designed to prioritize plants for control, to provide information to those working on habitat restoration, to show areas where research is needed, to aid those who prepare or comment on environmental planning documents, and to educate public policy makers. Plants that lack published information may be good starting points for student research projects. The Inventory cannot address, and is not intended to address, the range of geographic variation in California, nor the inherently regional nature of invasive species impacts. While we have noted where each plant is invasive, only the cumulative statewide impacts of the species have been considered in the evaluation. The impact of these plants in specific geographic regions or **habitats** within California may be greater or lesser than their statewide rating indicates. Management actions for a species should be considered on a local and site-specific basis, as the inventory does not attempt to suggest management needs for specific sites or regions. The criteria system was designed to be adapted at multiple scales, and local groups are encouraged to use the criteria for rating plants in their particular area.

Summary of the Criteria

17 The full Criteria, including explanations for scores for each question, are available at http://www.cal-ipc.org/ip/inventory/pdf/Criteria.pdf.

Section 1. Ecological Impact

18
1.1 Impact on abiotic ecosystem processes (e.g., hydrology, fire, nutrient cycling)
1.2 Impact on native plant community composition, structure, and interactions
1.3 Impact on higher trophic levels, including vertebrates and invertebrates
1.4 Impact on genetic integrity of native species (i.e., potential for hybridization)

Section 2. Invasive Potential

19
2.1 Ability to establish without anthropogenic or natural disturbance
2.2 Local rate of spread with no management
2.3 Recent trend in total area infested within state
2.4 Innate reproductive potential (based on multiple characteristics)
2.5 Potential for human-caused dispersal
2.6 Potential for natural long-distance (>1 km) dispersal
2.7 Other regions invaded worldwide that are similar to California

Section 3. Distribution

NOTES

20 3.1 Ecological amplitude (ecological types invaded in California)
3.2 Ecological intensity (highest extent of infestation in any one ecological type)

Documentation Levels

21 Assessed as highest level of documentation for each criterion.

22 4 = Reviewed scientific publications
3 = Other published material (reports or other non-peer-reviewed documents)
2 = Observational (unpublished information confirmed by a professional in the field)
1 = Anecdotal (unconfirmed information)
0 = No information

THINK QUESTIONS

CA-CCSS: CA.RI.7.1, CA.L.7.4a, CA.L.7.4b, CA.L.7.4c, CA.L.7.4d, CA.L.7.6, CA.SL.7.1b, CA.SL.7.1d, CA.SL.7.2, CA.SL.7.4

1. What is the purpose of the California Invasive Plant Inventory? Cite specific evidence from the report to support your response.

2. What limitations do people need to consider when using the Inventory to plan land-management actions in their own region of the state? Cite specific evidence from paragraphs 3 and 16 to support your understanding of the issue.

3. What is the structure of the criteria system used to rate plants? How are scores assigned to the plants? Cite specific evidence from paragraph 11 in your answer.

4. Use the context clues provided in the first paragraph to determine the meaning of **invasive** as it is used in the first sentence of the text. Write your definition of *invasive* and tell how you inferred the word's meaning. Then use a print or digital dictionary to verify the meaning of the word.

5. By recalling that *eco-* is a Greek combining form meaning "environment" or "habitat," that *-logy* is also a Greek combining form meaning "science," and that *-al* is a Latin suffix meaning "of," how can you use context clues and Greek and Latin roots and affixes to figure out the meaning of **ecological**, as it is used in the first paragraph? Write your definition of *ecological* and tell how you figured out the meaning of the word. Then use a general or specialized print or digital dictionary to determine the precise meaning of this scientific term.

CLOSE READ

CA-CCSS: CA.RI.7.1, CA.RI.7.2, CA.RI.7.4, CA.RI.7.5, CA.RI.7.5a, CA.L.7.4a, CA.L.7.4c, CA.L.7.6, CA.W.7.2a, CA.W.7.2b, CA.W.7.2c, CA.W.7.2d, CA.W.7.2e, CA.W.7.2f, CA.W.7.4, CA.W.7.5, CA.W.7.6, CA.W.7.9b, CA.W.7.10

Reread the text "California Invasive Plant Inventory." As you reread, complete the Focus Questions below. Then use your answers and annotations from the questions to help you complete the Writing Prompt.

FOCUS QUESTIONS

1. Reread paragraph 5. What technical terms are used in the paragraph? How can the reader go about finding the definitions of these words? Highlight the terms and make annotations to explain how you can figure out what they mean.

2. Reread paragraph 9. Highlight the central idea of the paragraph. Then make annotations to record the central idea.

3. The main text structure in paragraph 12 is description. What other text structure is used in the paragraph? Highlight textual evidence and make annotations to explain your reasoning.

4. Highlight the technical term *ecological amplitude* in paragraph 15. Make annotations to record a definition based on an online search. Cite your online source.

5. What are some of the central ideas, descriptions, and technical language used in paragraphs 2, 7, and 16 of "California Invasive Plant Inventory" that help address the question "What are the challenges of human interactions with the environment?" Highlight textual evidence and make annotations to support your answer.

WRITING PROMPT

How does the information in "California Invasive Plant Inventory" support the idea that human interactions affect the environment? Use your understanding of the selection's central or main ideas, text structures, and technical language to collect evidence for your analysis. Use the details you have collected to

- identify how human interactions contribute (or have contributed) to the spread of non-native invasive plants.
- identify how human interactions can help repair the damage of invasive plants.
- identify what role the Inventory plays in understanding the processes.

Begin with a clear thesis statement that makes a claim about your understanding of the information presented. Remember to support your writing with textual evidence and inferences, using precise language and technical terms from the selection to strengthen your ideas. Use transitions to show the relationships among your ideas, and establish a formal style to deliver your information. Provide a conclusion that successfully summarizes your central ideas and leaves the reader with a final thought regarding his or her own responsibility regarding the information you have presented.

THE DANGERS OF SOCIAL MEDIA

NON-FICTION

2015

INTRODUCTION

The writers of these two articles agree that social media has become an integral part of our lives, but they disagree on who should be using it. One writer argues that it may be helpful for preteens to gain experience in the world of social media, in order that they learn how to use it appropriately as teenagers and adults. The other writer argues that social media is fraught with dangers, and could have detrimental effects on young users. Both writers present strong arguments and support their claims with sound reasoning and convincing evidence. Which argument do you feel is more persuasive?

"Once something is posted on the Internet, it remains there forever."

FIRST READ

1 Social Media: Is it Safe for Preteens?

2 Point: Social Media Should Be Available to Preteens

3 In today's world, social media has become a tool with many uses. In addition to being a way for people to connect all over the world, websites such as Facebook and Twitter have become important ways for people to share useful information. By denying preteens access to social media, we are denying them access to a large amount of information. Currently, the Children's Online Privacy Protection Act (COPPA), created in 1998, prohibits children under the age of 13 from creating accounts on social media websites. Facebook, Twitter, Instagram, and Pinterest are off limits to kids under 13. This law is outdated and should be changed. Preteens should be allowed access to social media for a variety of reasons.

4 Because social media has become so **prevalent** in our society, it is important for adolescents to learn how to use these tools appropriately. By the time children reach the age of 11 or 12, they have already become quite aware of the **allure** of social media. Eleven is old enough for children to understand the consequences of their actions, both online and off. During the preteen years, children should begin participating in the world of social media so that they will be well prepared to interact in this world by the time they become teenagers and adults.

5 With appropriate adult supervision and guidance, preteens should have no trouble navigating the world of social media. Facebook is developing a version of the site that would allow special parental supervision for children under the age of 13. If children are aware that their parents can see everything they do, they are more likely to behave appropriately. Besides Facebook, there are already a lot of preteen-friendly social media sites that include

NOTES

parental controls. Many of these sites don't require much personal information in order to sign up.

6 Social media could be a good learning experience for preteens in other ways, too. Allowing preteens to use social media could be an effective way to educate them about privacy policies and Internet safety in a controlled environment. This is better than turning them loose without any guidance once they turn 13.

7 Social media can be helpful for children in a lot of ways. Interacting with others through websites such as Facebook and Twitter can be much easier for introverted kids than in-person interactions while providing the same benefits. Social media can also help create community among people who have things in common. For example, Facebook has several support groups for people who suffer from chronic illnesses such as epilepsy and diabetes. Preteens with these conditions might have trouble finding an in-person support group to join. Social media websites can provide the kind of supportive environment they need.

8 When we deny preteens access to social media, we deny them access to support groups, information, and a world of potential friends and learning experiences. It's time for COPPA to be updated to allow preteens to reap the benefits of all that social media has to offer them.

9 **Counterpoint: Social Media Is Dangerous for Preteens**

10 The world is becoming more and more fast-paced. The time that children are able to spend just being kids is shrinking all the time. Everyone knows that social media has become a huge part of our everyday lives. Facebook allows children as young as 13 to create accounts, even though there are currently no special provisions for parental supervision. The Internet is still in its infancy, and it can be a dangerous place for children. Preteens should not be allowed on social media websites.

11 The obesity epidemic in our nation is already a serious problem. Several programs have been instituted to get children exercising outdoors and away from the television set and the computer. Sanctioning social media usage for preteens would be adding just another obstacle to keeping preteens outdoors and active.

12 Facebook is working to launch a preteen-friendly, "training wheels" version of the website,. However, their main goal is to boost market share by increasing advertising **revenue**. What this means for preteens is that Facebook is more interested in advertising to them than in including them or teaching them how to use social media safely and effectively.

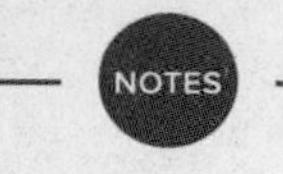

13 Preteens are highly **susceptible** to marketing that is targeted at them, and they are already exposed to plenty of advertising on television, billboards, computers, and even in some schools. It is important to minimize preteens' exposure to advertising wherever possible, and social media websites are often riddled with ads.

14 Along the same lines, preteens are also susceptible to body image and self-esteem issues. The reliance on photos and the shallowness of online relationships can foster these issues, lowering the self-worth of preteens. Most social media websites make it easy to use pictures instead of words to convey information, and this **superficial** approach to friendship can make it difficult for adolescents to form deeper relationships.

15 Of course, preteens can't be expected to have the foresight necessary to keep from posting words and images that might come back to haunt them later. People are especially sensitive to criticism and embarrassment during the preteen years. Something that might seem like a good idea to post one day might be a terrible idea the next. Once something is posted on the Internet, it remains there forever. Even after you take it down, it might resurface later—even if you don't want it to! We live in a world in which politicians can be brought down by a single photo unearthed from the Internet. Allowing preteens to upload information to the Internet is too risky for their future.

16 The advent of cyberbullying shows that preteens and even teenagers are often not quite mature enough to understand how their behavior can affect others. Cyberbullying is rampant among young Facebook users. Allowing even younger people to join this social website is likely to worsen the problem.

17 Social media has become a mainstay in our society, and it doesn't look as if it is going away anytime soon. Once children turn 13, they will have their entire lives to use social media—there's no reason to rush it. When the risks are so great, why not be patient?

THINK QUESTIONS

CA-CCSS: CA.RI.7.1, CA.L.7.4a, CA.L.7.4d

1. What evidence is there that both the "Point" and "Counterpoint" writers believe that social media is a permanent part of American society? What different conclusion do the writers draw from this point of view? Cite specific textual evidence to support your responses.

2. What does the Children's Online Privacy Protection Act (COPPA) prohibit? What view of COPPA does the "Point" writer hold? What evidence enables you to infer that the "Counterpoint" writer would not agree with the "Point" writer's point of view? Cite specific textual evidence to support your answer.

3. What is the "Point" writer's opinion about the ability of preteens to understand the consequences of online activities? What is the "Counterpoint" writer's point of view about this? Cite specific textual evidence to support your understanding.

4. Use the context clues in the second paragraph of the "Point" text to determine the meaning of **allure.** Write your definition of *allure* and tell how you figured out the meaning of the word. Then verify the meaning you inferred by checking it in a print or digital dictionary.

5. Use the context clues in the fifth paragraph of the "Counterpoint" text to determine the meaning of **superficial.** Write your definition of *superficial* and tell how you figured out the word's meaning. Then verify your definition of the word by checking it in context.

CLOSE READ

CA-CCSS: CA.RI.7.1, CA.RI.7.2, CA.RI.7.6, CA.RI.7.8, CA.RI.7.9, CA.W.7.1a, CA.W.7.1b, CA.W.7.1c, CA.W.7.1d, CA.W.7.1e, CA.W.7.4, CA.W.7.5, CA.W.7.6, CA.W.7.9b, CA.W.7.10

Reread the text "The Dangers of Social Media." As you reread, complete the Focus Questions below. Then use your answers and annotations from the questions to help you complete the Writing Prompt.

FOCUS QUESTIONS

1. How do the "Point" and "Counterpoint" writers use the first paragraph of their essays to establish their purpose and point of view? What are their different points of view about preteen access to social media? Highlight relevant textual evidence. Make annotations to analyze how the "Point" writer distinguishes his or her position from the "Counterpoint" writer as they argue two different sides of the same topic.
2. Reread the fourth paragraph of the "Point" argument to trace and evaluate the writer's claim. Highlight the claim the writer makes. Then make annotations to evaluate the claim.
3. Reread the second paragraph of the "Counterpoint" argument to trace and evaluate the writer's claim. Highlight the claim the writer makes. Then make annotations to evaluate the claim.
4. Reread the second paragraph of the "Point" argument and the seventh paragraph of the "Counterpoint" argument. Highlight the claims each writer makes to determine his or her point of view. Then make annotations to discuss how the two writers distinguish their positions.
5. How do the "Point" and "Counterpoint" writers address the challenges of human interactions in terms of preteen access to social media? How does the evidence they present reflect their differing points of view? Highlight textual evidence and make annotations to support your response.

WRITING PROMPT

You have read two opposing points of view in "The Dangers of Social Media." In your opinion, which author made the stronger argument? Why was the author you chose more convincing? Support your own writing with sound reasoning and relevant evidence from the text to explain why one author and not the other persuaded you to accept his or her point of view about why preteens should (or shouldn't) have access to social media. Use transitions to show the relationships among your ideas, and establish a formal style that addresses your topic appropriately. Provide a conclusion that summarizes your key information.

MY ÁNTONIA

FICTION

Willa Cather

1918

INTRODUCTION

Willa Cather was born in Back Creek Valley, Virginia in 1873, one of seven children. When she was six, her family traveled west to live at Cather's grandfather's farm in Nebraska, alongside many European pioneers. These early days helped inspire *My Ántonia*, a rhapsodic tale of a spirited young Bohemian woman making her way on the plains. In this chapter, the book's narrator, Jim Burden, acts to prove himself to Ántonia.

"...there, on one of those dry gravel beds, was the biggest snake I had ever seen."

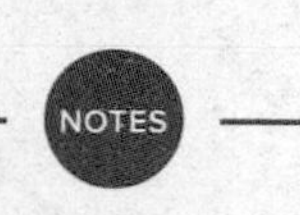

FIRST READ

Excerpt from Book I: The Shimerdas
Chapter VII

1 Much as I liked Ántonia, I hated a superior tone that she sometimes took with me. She was four years older than I, to be sure, and had seen more of the world; but I was a boy and she was a girl, and I resented her protecting manner. Before the autumn was over, she began to treat me more like an equal and to **defer** to me in other things than reading lessons. This change came about from an adventure we had together.

2 One day when I rode over to the Shimerdas' I found Ántonia starting off on foot for Russian Peter's house, to borrow a spade Ambrosch needed. I offered to take her on the pony, and she got up behind me. There had been another black frost the night before, and the air was clear and heady as wine. Within a week all the blooming roads had been despoiled, hundreds of miles of yellow sunflowers had been transformed into brown, rattling, burry stalks.

3 We found Russian Peter digging his potatoes. We were glad to go in and get warm by his kitchen stove and to see his squashes and Christmas melons, heaped in the storeroom for winter. As we rode away with the spade, Ántonia suggested that we stop at the prairie-dog-town and dig into one of the holes. We could find out whether they ran straight down, or were horizontal, like mole-holes; whether they had underground connections; whether the owls had nests down there, lined with feathers. We might get some puppies, or owl eggs, or snakeskins.

4 The dog-town was spread out over perhaps ten acres. The grass had been nibbled short and even, so this stretch was not shaggy and red like the surrounding country, but grey and velvety. The holes were several yards

NOTES

apart, and were disposed with a good deal of regularity, almost as if the town had been laid out in streets and avenues. One always felt that an orderly and very sociable kind of life was going on there. I picketed Dude down in a draw, and we went wandering about, looking for a hole that would be easy to dig. The dogs were out, as usual, dozens of them, sitting up on their hind legs over the doors of their houses. As we approached, they barked, shook their tails at us, and scurried underground. Before the mouths of the holes were little patches of sand and gravel, scratched up, we supposed, from a long way below the surface. Here and there, in the town, we came on larger gravel patches, several yards away from any hole. If the dogs had scratched the sand up in excavating, how had they carried it so far? It was on one of these gravel beds that I met my adventure.

5 We were examining a big hole with two entrances. The burrow sloped into the ground at a gentle angle, so that we could see where the two corridors united, and the floor was dusty from use, like a little highway over which much travel went. I was walking backward, in a crouching position, when I heard Ántonia scream. She was standing opposite me, pointing behind me and shouting something in Bohemian. I whirled round, and there, on one of those dry gravel beds, was the biggest snake I had ever seen. He was sunning himself, after the cold night, and he must have been asleep when Ántonia screamed. When I turned, he was lying in long loose waves, like a letter 'W.' He twitched and began to coil slowly. He was not merely a big snake, I thought—he was a circus monstrosity. His **abominable** muscularity, his **loathsome,** fluid motion, somehow made me sick. He was as thick as my leg, and looked as if millstones couldn't crush the disgusting vitality out of him. He lifted his hideous little head, and rattled. I didn't run because I didn't think of it—if my back had been against a stone wall I couldn't have felt more cornered. I saw his coils tighten—now he would spring, spring his length, I remembered. I ran up and drove at his head with my spade, struck him fairly across the neck, and in a minute he was all about my feet in wavy loops. I struck now from hate. Ántonia, barefooted as she was, ran up behind me. Even after I had pounded his ugly head flat, his body kept on coiling and winding, doubling and falling back on itself. I walked away and turned my back. I felt seasick.

6 Ántonia came after me, crying, 'O Jimmy, he not bite you? You sure? Why you not run when I say?'

7 'What did you jabber Bohunk for? You might have told me there was a snake behind me!' I said petulantly.

8 'I know I am just awful, Jim, I was so scared.' She took my handkerchief from my pocket and tried to wipe my face with it, but I snatched it away from her. I suppose I looked as sick as I felt.

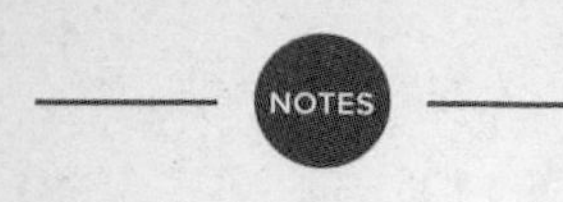

9 'I never know you was so brave, Jim,' she went on comfortingly. 'You is just like big mans; you wait for him lift his head and then you go for him. Ain't you feel scared a bit? Now we take that snake home and show everybody. Nobody ain't seen in this kawntree so big snake like you kill.'

10 She went on in this strain until I began to think that I had longed for this opportunity, and had hailed it with joy. Cautiously we went back to the snake; he was still groping with his tail, turning up his ugly belly in the light. A faint, fetid smell came from him, and a thread of green liquid oozed from his crushed head.

11 'Look, Tony, that's his poison,' I said.

12 I took a long piece of string from my pocket, and she lifted his head with the spade while I tied a noose around it. We pulled him out straight and measured him by my riding-quirt; he was about five and a half feet long. He had twelve rattles, but they were broken off before they began to taper, so I insisted that he must once have had twenty-four. I explained to Ántonia how this meant that he was twenty-four years old, that he must have been there when white men first came, left on from buffalo and Indian times. As I turned him over, I began to feel proud of him, to have a kind of respect for his age and size. He seemed like the ancient, eldest Evil. Certainly his kind have left horrible unconscious memories in all warm-blooded life. When we dragged him down into the draw, Dude sprang off to the end of his tether and shivered all over—wouldn't let us come near him.

13 We decided that Ántonia should ride Dude home, and I would walk. As she rode along slowly, her bare legs swinging against the pony's sides, she kept shouting back to me about how astonished everybody would be. I followed with the spade over my shoulder, dragging my snake. Her exultation was contagious. The great land had never looked to me so big and free. If the red grass were full of rattlers, I was equal to them all. Nevertheless, I stole furtive glances behind me now and then to see that no avenging mate, older and bigger than my quarry, was racing up from the rear.

14 The sun had set when we reached our garden and went down the draw toward the house. Otto Fuchs was the first one we met. He was sitting on the edge of the cattle-pond, having a quiet pipe before supper. Ántonia called him to come quick and look. He did not say anything for a minute, but scratched his head and turned the snake over with his boot.

15 'Where did you run onto that beauty, Jim?'

16 'Up at the dog-town,' I answered **laconically.**

17 'Kill him yourself? How come you to have a weepon?'

18 'We'd been up to Russian Peter's, to borrow a spade for Ambrosch.'

19 Otto shook the ashes out of his pipe and squatted down to count the rattles. 'It was just luck you had a tool,' he said cautiously. 'Gosh! I wouldn't want to do any business with that fellow myself, unless I had a fence-post along. Your grandmother's snake-cane wouldn't more than tickle him. He could stand right up and talk to you, he could. Did he fight hard?'

20 Ántonia broke in: 'He fight something awful! He is all over Jimmy's boots. I scream for him to run, but he just hit and hit that snake like he was crazy.'

21 Otto winked at me. After Ántonia rode on he said: 'Got him in the head first crack, didn't you? That was just as well.'

22 We hung him up to the windmill, and when I went down to the kitchen, I found Ántonia standing in the middle of the floor, telling the story with a great deal of color.

23 Subsequent experiences with rattlesnakes taught me that my first encounter was fortunate in circumstance. My big rattler was old, and had led too easy a life; there was not much fight in him. He had probably lived there for years, with a fat prairie-dog for breakfast whenever he felt like it, a sheltered home, even an owl-feather bed, perhaps, and he had forgot that the world doesn't owe rattlers a living. A snake of his size, in fighting trim, would be more than any boy could handle. So in reality it was a mock adventure; the game was fixed for me by chance, as it probably was for many a dragon-slayer. I had been adequately armed by Russian Peter; the snake was old and lazy; and I had Ántonia beside me, to appreciate and admire.

24 That snake hung on our corral fence for several days; some of the neighbors came to see it and agreed that it was the biggest rattler ever killed in those parts. This was enough for Ántonia. She liked me better from that time on, and she never took a **supercilious** air with me again. I had killed a big snake—I was now a big fellow.

THINK QUESTIONS CA-CCSS: CA.RL.7.1, CA.RL.7.4, CA.L.7.4a, CA.L.7.4b, CA.L.7.4d

1. Refer to one or more details from the text to describe Jim and Ántonia's relationship before the incident with the rattlesnake. Use evidence that is directly stated and inferences that you draw from clues in the text.

2. Use details from the text to write two or three sentences to describe Jims reaction to the rattlesnake he encounters in the prairie-dog-town.

3. Write several sentences explaining how the incident with the rattlesnake changes the relationship between Jim and Ántonia. Support your answer with specific evidence from the text.

4. Use context to determine the meaning of the word **laconically** as it is used in paragraph 16 of *My Ántonia*. Write your definition of *laconically* and tell how you figured out the meaning of the word. Then verify the meaning in a print or digital dictionary.

5. Noting that the Latin prefix *super-* means "above or beyond" and the Latin root *cilium* means "eyebrow," use the context clues provided in the passage to determine the meaning of **supercilious** in the last paragraph. Write your definition of *supercilious* and tell how you determined the meaning of the word.

CLOSE READ

CA-CCSS: CA.RL.7.1, CA.RL.7.2, CA.RL.7.3, CA.W.7.2a, CA.W.7.2b, CA.W.7.2c, CA.W.7.2d, CA.W.7.2e, CA.W.7.2f

Reread the excerpt from *My Ántonia*. As you reread, complete the Focus Questions below. Then use your answers and annotations from the questions to help you complete the Writing Prompt.

FOCUS QUESTIONS

1. In paragraph 2, what evidence is there that the natural and historical setting of the American West in the nineteenth century is a source of conflict for the settlers who are looking for a better way of life? Highlight textual evidence. Make annotations to explain the negative effects of the setting on the characters.
2. In paragraph 3, what evidence is there that the setting of the American West offers opportunity for immigrants such as Ántonia's family and Russian Peter? Highlight textual evidence and make annotations to explain your analysis.
3. How does Jim's encounter with the rattlesnake in the prairie-dog-town illustrate the conflict presented by the setting, in paragraph 5? Highlight textual evidence and make annotations to explain your ideas.
4. In what ways does the setting influence Jim's passage into adulthood? Highlight textual evidence in paragraphs 5 and 24. Then make annotations to explain how this evidence supports your analysis.
5. How does Ántonia's status as a girl and an immigrant and Jim's status as a boy and a native-born American create challenges for them as they interact with each other? Highlight textual evidence and make annotations to support your response.

WRITING PROMPT

How does the setting of *My Ántonia* contribute to the challenges Jim faces in his interactions with Ántonia? Use the details you have compiled from examining the setting and characters to

- identify the natural and historical conditions of the setting that help shape the characters and the way they interact.
- identify how and why the characters' interactions change over the course of the story.

Begin with a clear thesis statement. Remember to organize and to support your writing with textual evidence and inferences, using precise language and selection vocabulary. Include transitions to show the relationships among your main ideas, and establish a formal style of delivery. Provide a conclusion that effectively summarizes your key information.

FREAK THE MIGHTY

FICTION

Rodman Philbrick

1993

INTRODUCTION

studysync tv

Max Kane, a learning-impaired adolescent of giant proportions, is called "Mad Max" and taunted relentlessly about his father, Killer Kane, in jail for murdering Max's mother. Max hates school, and prefers the seclusion of his basement room...until a new boy moves in next door. Self-dubbed "the Freak" due to a genetically malformed body, Kevin is Max's opposite—bright, energetic and curious. Together, they become Freak the Mighty, and embark on a series of adventures.

"...this midget kid, this crippled little humanoid, he actually scared you."

FIRST READ

NOTES

Chapter Three: American Flyer

1 OK, back to the down under, right? My room in the basement. Scuttle into your dim hole in the ground, Maxwell dear. Big goon like you, growing about an inch a day, and this midget kid, this crippled little humanoid, he actually *scared* you. Not the kind of scare that makes your knee bones feel like water, more the kind of scare where you go whoa! I don't understand this, I don't get it, what's going on?

2 Like calling me "earthling." Which by itself is pretty weird, right? I already mentioned a few of the names I've been called, but until the robot boy showed up, nobody had ever called me *earthling,* and so I'm lying on my mattress there in the great down under, and it comes to me that he's right, I *am* an earthling, we're all of us earthlings, but we don't call each other earthling. No need. Because it's the same thing that in this country we're all Americans, but we don't go around to people and say, "Excuse me, American, can you tell me how to get to the nearest 7 Eleven?"

3 So I'm thinking about that for a while, lying there in the cellar dark, and pretty soon the down under starts to get small, like the walls are shrinking, and I go up the bulkhead stairs into the back yard and find a place where I can check it out.

4 There's this one scraggly tree behind the little freak's house, right? Like a stick in the ground with a few wimped out branches. And there he is, hardly any bigger now than he was in day care, and he's standing there waving his crutch up at the tree.

5 I kind of slide over to the chain-link fence, get a better angle on the scene. What's he *doing* whacking at that crummy tree? Trying to jump up and hit this branch with his little crutch, and he's mad, hopping mad. Only he can't really

jump, he just makes this jumping kind of motion. His feet never leave the ground.

6 Then what he does, he throws down the crutch and he gets down on his hands and knees and crawls back to his house. If you didn't know, you would think he was like a kindergarten creeper who forgot how to walk, he's that small. And he crawls real good, better than he can walk. Before you know it, he's dragging this wagon out from under the steps.

7 Rusty red thing, one of those old American Flyer models. Anyhow, the little freak is tugging it backwards, a few inches at a time. Chugging along until he gets that little wagon under the tree. Next thing he picks up his crutch and he climbs in the wagon and he stands up and he's whacking at the tree again.

8 By now I've figured out that there's something stuck up in the branches and he wants to get it down. This small, bright-colored thing, looks like a piece of folded paper. Whatever it is, that paper thing, he wants it real bad, but even with the wagon there's no way he can reach it. No way.

9 So I go over there to his back yard, trying to be real quiet, but I'm not good at sneaking up, not with these **humongous** feet, and he turns and faces me with that crutch raised up like he's ready to hit a grand slam on my head.

10 He wants to say something, you can tell that much, but he's so mad, he's all huffed up and the noise he makes, it could be from a dog or something, and he sounds like he can hardly breathe.

11 What I do, I keep out of range of that crutch and just reach up and pick the paper thing right out of the tree. Except it's not a paper thing. It's a plastic bird, light as a feather. I have to hold it real careful or it might break, that's how flimsy it is.

12 I go, "You want this back or what?"

13 The little freak is staring at me bug-eyed, and he goes, "Oh, it talks."

14 I give him the bird-thing. "What is it, like a model airplane or something?"

15 You can tell he's real happy to have the bird-thing back, and his face isn't quite so fierce. He sits down in the wagon and he goes, "This is an ornithopter. An ornithopter is defined as an experimental device propelled by flapping wings. Or you could say that an ornithopter is just a big word for mechanical bird."

16 That's how he talked, like right out of a dictionary. So smart you can hardly believe it. While he's talking he's winding up the bird-thing. There's this elastic band inside, and he goes, "Observe and be amazed, earthling," and then he

lets it go, and you know what? I *am* amazed, because it does fly around like a little bird, flitting up and down and around, higher than I can reach.

17 I chase after the thing until it boinks against the scrawny tree trunk and I bring it back to him and he winds it up again and makes it fly. We keep doing that, it must be for almost an hour, until finally the elastic breaks. I figure that's it, end of ornithopter, but he says something like, "All mechanical objects require **periodic maintenance.** We'll schedule **installation** of a new **propulsion** unit as soon as the Fair Gwen of Air gets a replacement."

18 Even though I'm not sure what he means, I go, "That's cool."

19 "You live around here, earthling?"

20 "Over there." I point out the house. "In the down under."

21 He goes, "What?" and I figure it's easier to show him than explain all about Gram and Grim and the room in the cellar, so I pick up the handle to the American Flyer wagon and I tow him over.

22 It's real easy, he doesn't weigh much and I'm pretty sure I remember looking back and seeing him sitting up in the wagon happy as can be, like he's really enjoying the ride and not embarrassed to have me pulling him around.

23 But like Freak says later in this book, you can remember anything, whether it happened or not. All I'm really sure of is he never hit me with that crutch.

Excerpted from *Freak the Mighty* by Rodman Philbrick, published by Scholastic Inc.

THINK QUESTIONS

CA-CCSS: CA.RL.7.1, CA.RL.7.4, CA.L.7.4a, CA.L.7.4b, CA.L.7.4d, CA.SL.7.1a, CA.SL.7.1c, CA.SL.7.3, CA.SL.7.4

1. Refer to one or more details from the text to describe how Maxwell (the larger boy) reacts to Kevin (the smaller boy) upon first meeting him—both from evidence that is directly stated and from ideas that you infer from clues in the text.

2. Use details to explain how Maxwell confronts his fear of Kevin. Cite specific evidence from paragraphs 3, 5, and 11.

3. Write two or three sentences explaining how Maxwell and Kevin begin a friendship. Include evidence from the text to support your explanation.

4. Use context clues to determine the meaning of the word **humongous** as it is used in paragraph 9 of *Freak the Mighty.* Write your definition of *humongous* and tell how you determined the meaning of the word.

5. By remembering that the Latin prefix *pro-* means "forward" and the Latin root *pellere* means "to drive," use the context clues provided in paragraph 17 to determine the meaning of **propulsion,** the noun form of the verb *propel,* although in this context it is being used as an adjective: *propulsion unit.* Write your definition of *propulsion* and tell how you figured out the word's meaning. Then verify your definition in a print or digital dictionary.

CLOSE READ

CA-CCSS: CA.RL.7.1, CA.RL.7.2, CA.RL.7.7, CA.W.7.2a, CA.W.7.2b, CA.W.7.2c, CA.W.7.2d, CA.W.7.2e, CA.W.7.2f, CA.W.7.4, CA.W.7.5, CA.W.7.6, CA.W.7.9a, CA.W.7.10

Reread the excerpt from *Freak the Mighty*. As you reread, complete the Focus Questions below. Then use your answers and annotations from the questions to help you complete the Writing Prompt.

FOCUS QUESTIONS

1. Listen to the audio recording of paragraph 3 (1:21–1:42). How does the actor use pacing when saying "walls" to suggest the action of shrinking walls? Highlight textual evidence in paragraph 3 and annotate ideas from the audio recording to show the development of your understanding of media techniques.

2. Listen to the audio recording of paragraph 4 (1:43–2:01). How does the actor use expression when he reads "day care" to convey his impressions of Kevin? Highlight textual evidence in paragraph 4 and annotate ideas from the audio recording to show the development of your understanding of media techniques.

3. Listen to the audio recording of paragraph 5 (2:02–2:28). How does the actor use intonation when he reads, "What's he *doing* whacking at that crummy tree?" and "hopping mad" to convey his attitude toward Kevin? Highlight textual evidence in paragraph 5 and annotate ideas from the audio recording to show the development of your understanding of media techniques.

4. Reread the last two paragraphs of the selection and then listen to the audio recording of the same paragraphs. Use details from the audio version and the printed text to explain what the actor in the audio narration adds to the reader's understanding of the story.

5. In what ways do Maxwell and Kevin experience challenges in their initial interactions? How do they overcome these challenges? Highlight textual evidence and make annotations to support your response.

WRITING PROMPT

Compare and contrast the text and audio versions *of Freak the Mighty.* How are the two versions alike, and how are they different? At what points does the audio version use expression, intonation, or pace to support or interpret the text? In what ways are these interpretations important or unimportant to the development of character, setting, plot, and theme? Begin with a clear thesis statement explaining your topic. Organize and support your writing with evidence from the text and audio file, using precise language, selection vocabulary, and a formal writing style. Include transitions to convey the relationships among your main points or ideas and provide a conclusion that summarizes your key information.

THE RANSOM OF RED CHIEF

FICTION

O. Henry
1910

INTRODUCTION

William Sydney Porter, who wrote under the pen name, O. Henry, was a prolific author, composing more than 600 short stories in his lifetime. An incisive social critic and witty raconteur, O. Henry is most famous for finishing his short stories with comic or ironic twists. This story about two men who pick the wrong boy to kidnap doesn't disappoint.

"Red Chief was sitting on Bill's chest, with one hand twined in Bill's hair."

FIRST READ

1 It looked like a good thing: but wait till I tell you. We were down South, in Alabama—Bill Driscoll and myself—when this kidnapping idea struck us. It was, as Bill afterward expressed it, "during a moment of temporary mental apparition"; but we didn't find that out till later.

2 There was a town down there, as flat as a flannel-cake, and called Summit, of course. It contained inhabitants of as undeleterious and self-satisfied a class of peasantry as ever clustered around a Maypole.

3 Bill and me had a joint capital of about six hundred dollars, and we needed just two thousand dollars more to pull off a fraudulent town-lot scheme in Western Illinois with. We talked it over on the front steps of the hotel. **Philoprogenitiveness**, says we, is strong in semi-rural communities; therefore and for other reasons, a kidnapping project ought to do better there than in the radius of newspapers that send reporters out in plain clothes to stir up talk about such things. We knew that Summit couldn't get after us with anything stronger than constables and maybe some lackadaisical bloodhounds and a diatribe or two in the Weekly Farmers' Budget. So, it looked good.

4 We selected for our victim the only child of a prominent citizen named Ebenezer Dorset. The father was respectable and tight, a mortgage fancier and a stern, upright collection-plate passer and forecloser. The kid was a boy of ten, with bas-relief freckles, and hair the colour of the cover of the magazine you buy at the news-stand when you want to catch a train. Bill and me figured that Ebenezer would melt down for a ransom of two thousand dollars to a cent. But wait till I tell you.

5 About two miles from Summit was a little mountain, covered with a dense cedar brake. On the rear elevation of this mountain was a cave. There we

NOTES

stored provisions. One evening after sundown, we drove in a buggy past old Dorset's house. The kid was in the street, throwing rocks at a kitten on the opposite fence.

6 "Hey, little boy!" says Bill, "would you like to have a bag of candy and a nice ride?"

7 The boy catches Bill neatly in the eye with a piece of brick.

8 "That will cost the old man an extra five hundred dollars," says Bill, climbing over the wheel.

9 That boy put up a fight like a welter-weight cinnamon bear; but, at last, we got him down in the bottom of the buggy and drove away. We took him up to the cave and I hitched the horse in the cedar brake. After dark I drove the buggy to the little village, three miles away, where we had hired it, and walked back to the mountain.

10 Bill was pasting court-plaster over the scratches and bruises on his features. There was a fire burning behind the big rock at the entrance of the cave, and the boy was watching a pot of boiling coffee, with two buzzard tail-feathers stuck in his red hair. He points a stick at me when I come up, and says:

11 "Ha! cursed paleface, do you dare to enter the camp of Red Chief, the terror of the plains?"

12 "He's all right now," says Bill, rolling up his trousers and examining some bruises on his shins. "We're playing Indian. We're making Buffalo Bill's show look like magic-lantern views of Palestine in the town hall. I'm Old Hank, the Trapper, Red Chief's captive, and I'm to be scalped at daybreak. By Geronimo! that kid can kick hard."

13 Yes, sir, that boy seemed to be having the time of his life. The fun of camping out in a cave had made him forget that he was a captive himself. He immediately christened me Snake-eye, the Spy, and announced that, when his braves returned from the warpath, I was to be broiled at the stake at the rising of the sun.

14 Then we had supper; and he filled his mouth full of bacon and bread and gravy, and began to talk. He made a during-dinner speech something like this:

15 "I like this fine. I never camped out before; but I had a pet 'possum once, and I was nine last birthday. I hate to go to school. Rats ate up sixteen of Jimmy Talbot's aunt's speckled hen's eggs. Are there any real Indians in these woods? I want some more gravy. Does the trees moving make the wind blow? We had five puppies. What makes your nose so red, Hank? My father has lots

of money. Are the stars hot? I whipped Ed Walker twice, Saturday. I don't like girls. You dassent catch toads unless with a string. Do oxen make any noise? Why are oranges round? Have you got beds to sleep on in this cave? Amos Murray has got six toes. A parrot can talk, but a monkey or a fish can't. How many does it take to make twelve?"

16 Every few minutes he would remember that he was a pesky Indian, and pick up his stick rifle and tiptoe to the mouth of the cave to rubber for the scouts of the hated paleface. Now and then he would let out a war-whoop that made Old Hank the Trapper shiver. That boy had Bill terrorized from the start.

17 "Red Chief," says I to the kid, "would you like to go home?"

18 "Aw, what for?" says he. "I don't have any fun at home. I hate to go to school. I like to camp out. You won't take me back home again, Snake-eye, will you?"

19 "Not right away," says I. "We'll stay here in the cave a while."

20 "All right!" says he. "That'll be fine. I never had such fun in all my life."

21 We went to bed about eleven o'clock. We spread down some wide blankets and quilts and put Red Chief between us. We weren't afraid he'd run away. He kept us awake for three hours, jumping up and reaching for his rifle and screeching: "Hist! pard," in mine and Bill's ears, as the fancied crackle of a twig or the rustle of a leaf revealed to his young imagination the stealthy approach of the outlaw band. At last, I fell into a troubled sleep, and dreamed that I had been kidnapped and chained to a tree by a **ferocious** pirate with red hair.

22 Just at daybreak, I was awakened by a series of awful screams from Bill. They weren't yells, or howls, or shouts, or whoops, or yawps, such as you'd expect from a manly set of vocal organs—they were simply indecent, terrifying, humiliating screams, such as women emit when they see ghosts or caterpillars. It's an awful thing to hear a strong, desperate, fat man scream incontinently in a cave at daybreak.

23 I jumped up to see what the matter was. Red Chief was sitting on Bill's chest, with one hand twined in Bill's hair. In the other he had the sharp case-knife we used for slicing bacon; and he was industriously and realistically trying to take Bill's scalp, according to the sentence that had been pronounced upon him the evening before.

24 I got the knife away from the kid and made him lie down again. But, from that moment, Bill's spirit was broken. He laid down on his side of the bed, but he never closed an eye again in sleep as long as that boy was with us. I dozed off for a while, but along toward sun-up I remembered that Red Chief had said

NOTES

I was to be burned at the stake at the rising of the sun. I wasn't nervous or afraid; but I sat up and lit my pipe and leaned against a rock.

25 "What you getting up so soon for, Sam?" asked Bill.

26 "Me?" says I. "Oh, I got a kind of a pain in my shoulder. I thought sitting up would rest it."

27 "You're a liar!" says Bill. "You're afraid. You was to be burned at sunrise, and you was afraid he'd do it. And he would, too, if he could find a match. Ain't it awful, Sam? Do you think anybody will pay out money to get a little imp like that back home?"

28 "Sure," said I. "A rowdy kid like that is just the kind that parents dote on. Now, you and the Chief get up and cook breakfast, while I go up on the top of this mountain and **reconnoitre.**"

29 I went up on the peak of the little mountain and ran my eye over the contiguous vicinity. Over toward Summit I expected to see the sturdy yeomanry of the village armed with scythes and pitchforks beating the countryside for the dastardly kidnappers. But what I saw was a peaceful landscape dotted with one man ploughing with a dun mule. Nobody was dragging the creek; no couriers dashed hither and yon, bringing tidings of no news to the distracted parents. There was a sylvan attitude of somnolent sleepiness pervading that section of the external outward surface of Alabama that lay exposed to my view. "Perhaps," says I to myself, "it has not yet been discovered that the wolves have borne away the tender lambkin from the fold. Heaven help the wolves!" says I, and I went down the mountain to breakfast.

30 When I got to the cave I found Bill backed up against the side of it, breathing hard, and the boy threatening to smash him with a rock half as big as a cocoanut.

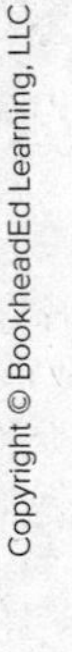

31 "He put a red-hot boiled potato down my back," explained Bill, "and then mashed it with his foot; and I boxed his ears. Have you got a gun about you, Sam?"

32 I took the rock away from the boy and kind of patched up the argument. "I'll fix you," says the kid to Bill. "No man ever yet struck the Red Chief but what he got paid for it. You better beware!"

33 After breakfast the kid takes a piece of leather with strings wrapped around it out of his pocket and goes outside the cave unwinding it.

34 "What's he up to now?" says Bill, anxiously. "You don't think he'll run away, do you, Sam?"

35 "No fear of it," says I. "He don't seem to be much of a home body. But we've got to fix up some plan about the ransom. There don't seem to be much excitement around Summit on account of his disappearance; but maybe they haven't realized yet that he's gone. His folks may think he's spending the night with Aunt Jane or one of the neighbours. Anyhow, he'll be missed to-day. To-night we must get a message to his father demanding the two thousand dollars for his return."

36 Just then we heard a kind of war-whoop, such as David might have emitted when he knocked out the champion Goliath. It was a sling that Red Chief had pulled out of his pocket, and he was whirling it around his head.

37 I dodged, and heard a heavy thud and a kind of a sigh from Bill, like a horse gives out when you take his saddle off. A rock the size of an egg had caught Bill just behind his left ear. He loosened himself all over and fell in the fire across the frying pan of hot water for washing the dishes. I dragged him out and poured cold water on his head for half an hour.

38 By and by, Bill sits up and feels behind his ear and says: "Sam, do you know who my favourite Biblical character is?"

39 "Take it easy," says I. "You'll come to your senses presently."

40 "King Herod," says he. "You won't go away and leave me here alone, will you, Sam?"

41 I went out and caught that boy and shook him until his freckles rattled.

42 "If you don't behave," says I, "I'll take you straight home. Now, are you going to be good, or not?"

43 "I was only funning," says he sullenly. "I didn't mean to hurt Old Hank. But what did he hit me for? I'll behave, Snake-eye, if you won't send me home, and if you'll let me play the Black Scout to-day."

44 "I don't know the game,' says I. "That's for you and Mr. Bill to decide. He's your playmate for the day. I'm going away for a while, on business. Now, you come in and make friends with him and say you are sorry for hurting him, or home you go, at once."

45 I made him and Bill shake hands, and then I took Bill aside and told him I was going to Poplar Cove, a little village three miles from the cave, and find out what I could about how the kidnapping had been regarded in Summit. Also, I thought it best to send a peremptory letter to old man Dorset that day, demanding the ransom and dictating how it should be paid.

NOTES

46 "You know, Sam," says Bill, "I've stood by you without batting an eye in earthquakes, fire and flood—in poker games, dynamite outrages, police raids, train robberies and cyclones. I never lost my nerve yet till we kidnapped that two-legged skyrocket of a kid. He's got me going. You won't leave me long with him, will you, Sam?"

47 "I'll be back some time this afternoon," says I. "You must keep the boy amused and quiet till I return. And now we'll write the letter to old Dorset."

48 Bill and I got paper and pencil and worked on the letter while Red Chief, with a blanket wrapped around him, strutted up and down, guarding the mouth of the cave. Bill begged me tearfully to make the ransom fifteen hundred dollars instead of two thousand. "I ain't attempting," says he, "to decry the celebrated moral aspect of parental affection, but we're dealing with humans, and it ain't human for anybody to give up two thousand dollars for that forty-pound chunk of freckled wildcat. I'm willing to take a chance at fifteen hundred dollars. You can charge the difference up to me."

49 So, to relieve Bill, I **acceded,** and we collaborated a letter that ran this way:

50 Ebenezer Dorset, Esq.:

51 We have your boy concealed in a place far from Summit. It is useless for you or the most skilful detectives to attempt to find him. Absolutely, the only terms on which you can have him restored to you are these: We demand fifteen hundred dollars in large bills for his return; the money to be left at midnight to-night at the same spot and in the same box as your reply—as hereinafter described. If you agree to these terms, send your answer in writing by a solitary messenger to-night at half-past eight o'clock. After crossing Owl Creek, on the road to Poplar Cove, there are three large trees about a hundred yards apart, close to the fence of the wheat field on the right-hand side. At the bottom of the fence-post, opposite the third tree, will be found a small pasteboard box.

52 The messenger will place the answer in this box and return immediately to Summit.

53 If you attempt any treachery or fail to comply with our demand as stated, you will never see your boy again.

54 If you pay the money as demanded, he will be returned to you safe and well within three hours. These terms are final, and if you do not accede to them no further communication will be attempted.

TWO DESPERATE MEN.

NOTES

55 I addressed this letter to Dorset, and put it in my pocket. As I was about to start, the kid comes up to me and says:

56 "Aw, Snake-eye, you said I could play the Black Scout while you was gone."

57 "Play it, of course," says I. "Mr. Bill will play with you. What kind of a game is it?"

58 "I'm the Black Scout," says Red Chief, "and I have to ride to the stockade to warn the settlers that the Indians are coming. I'm tired of playing Indian myself. I want to be the Black Scout."

59 "All right," says I. "It sounds harmless to me. I guess Mr. Bill will help you foil the pesky Indians."

60 "What am I to do?" asks Bill, looking at the kid suspiciously.

61 "You are the hoss," says Black Scout. "Get down on your hands and knees. How can I ride to the stockade without a hoss?"

62 "You'd better keep him interested," said I, "till we get the scheme going. Loosen up."

63 Bill gets down on his all fours, and a look comes in his eye like a rabbit's when you catch it in a trap.

64 "How far is it to the stockade, kid?" he asks, in a husky manner of voice.

65 "Ninety miles," says the Black Scout. "And you have to hump yourself to get there on time. Whoa, now!"

66 The Black Scout jumps on Bill's back and digs his heels in his side.

67 "For Heaven's sake," says Bill, "hurry back, Sam, as soon as you can. I wish we hadn't made the ransom more than a thousand. Say, you quit kicking me or I'll get up and warm you good."

68 I walked over to Poplar Cove and sat around the postoffice and store, talking with the chawbacons that came in to trade. One whiskerando says that he hears Summit is all upset on account of Elder Ebenezer Dorset's boy having been lost or stolen. That was all I wanted to know. I bought some smoking tobacco, referred casually to the price of black-eyed peas, posted my letter surreptitiously and came away. The postmaster said the mail-carrier would come by in an hour to take the mail on to Summit.

69 When I got back to the cave Bill and the boy were not to be found. I explored the vicinity of the cave, and risked a yodel or two, but there was no response.

70 So I lighted my pipe and sat down on a mossy bank to await developments.

71 In about half an hour I heard the bushes rustle, and Bill wabbled out into the little glade in front of the cave. Behind him was the kid, stepping softly like a scout, with a broad grin on his face. Bill stopped, took off his hat and wiped his face with a red handkerchief. The kid stopped about eight feet behind him.

72 "Sam," says Bill, "I suppose you'll think I'm a renegade, but I couldn't help it. I'm a grown person with masculine proclivities and habits of self-defense, but there is a time when all systems of egotism and predominance fail. The boy is gone. I have sent him home. All is off. There was martyrs in old times," goes on Bill, "that suffered death rather than give up the particular graft they enjoyed. None of 'em ever was subjugated to such supernatural tortures as I have been. I tried to be faithful to our articles of depredation; but there came a limit."

73 "What's the trouble, Bill?" I asks him.

74 "I was rode," says Bill, "the ninety miles to the stockade, not barring an inch. Then, when the settlers was rescued, I was given oats. Sand ain't a palatable substitute. And then, for an hour I had to try to explain to him why there was nothin' in holes, how a road can run both ways and what makes the grass green. I tell you, Sam, a human can only stand so much. I takes him by the neck of his clothes and drags him down the mountain. On the way he kicks my legs black-and-blue from the knees down; and I've got to have two or three bites on my thumb and hand cauterized.

75 "But he's gone"—continues Bill—"gone home. I showed him the road to Summit and kicked him about eight feet nearer there at one kick. I'm sorry we lose the ransom; but it was either that or Bill Driscoll to the madhouse."

76 Bill is puffing and blowing, but there is a look of ineffable peace and growing content on his rose-pink features.

77 "Bill," says I, "there isn't any heart disease in your family, is there?"

78 "No," says Bill, "nothing chronic except malaria and accidents. Why?"

79 "Then you might turn around," says I, "and have a look behind you."

80 Bill turns and sees the boy, and loses his complexion and sits down plump on the round and begins to pluck aimlessly at grass and little sticks. For an hour I was afraid for his mind. And then I told him that my scheme was to put the whole job through immediately and that we would get the ransom and be off with it by midnight if old Dorset fell in with our proposition. So Bill braced up

enough to give the kid a weak sort of a smile and a promise to play the Russian in a Japanese war with him as soon as he felt a little better.

81 I had a scheme for collecting that ransom without danger of being caught by counterplots that ought to commend itself to professional kidnappers. The tree under which the answer was to be left—and the money later on—was close to the road fence with big, bare fields on all sides. If a gang of constables should be watching for any one to come for the note they could see him a long way off crossing the fields or in the road. But no, sirree! At half-past eight I was up in that tree as well hidden as a tree toad, waiting for the messenger to arrive.

82 Exactly on time, a half-grown boy rides up the road on a bicycle, locates the pasteboard box at the foot of the fence-post, slips a folded piece of paper into it and pedals away again back toward Summit.

83 I waited an hour and then concluded the thing was square. I slid down the tree, got the note, slipped along the fence till I struck the woods, and was back at the cave in another half an hour. I opened the note, got near the lantern and read it to Bill. It was written with a pen in a crabbed hand, and the sum and substance of it was this:

84 Two Desperate Men.

85 Gentlemen: I received your letter to-day by post, in regard to the ransom you ask for the return of my son. I think you are a little high in your demands, and I hereby make you a counter-proposition, which I am inclined to believe you will accept. You bring Johnny home and pay me two hundred and fifty dollars in cash, and I agree to take him off your hands. You had better come at night, for the neighbours believe he is lost, and I couldn't be responsible for what they would do to anybody they saw bringing him back. Very respectfully,

86 EBENEZER DORSET.

87 "Great pirates of Penzance!" says I; "of all the **impudent—**"

88 But I glanced at Bill, and hesitated. He had the most appealing look in his eyes I ever saw on the face of a dumb or a talking brute.

89 "Sam," says he, "what's two hundred and fifty dollars, after all? We've got the money. One more night of this kid will send me to a bed in Bedlam. Besides being a thorough gentleman, I think Mr. Dorset is a spendthrift for making us such a liberal offer. You ain't going to let the chance go, are you?"

90 "Tell you the truth, Bill," says I, "this little he ewe lamb has somewhat got on my nerves too. We'll take him home, pay the ransom and make our get-away."

91 We took him home that night. We got him to go by telling him that his father had bought a silver-mounted rifle and a pair of moccasins for him, and we were going to hunt bears the next day.

92 It was just twelve o'clock when we knocked at Ebenezer's front door. Just at the moment when I should have been abstracting the fifteen hundred dollars from the box under the tree, according to the original proposition, Bill was counting out two hundred and fifty dollars into Dorset's hand.

93 When the kid found out we were going to leave him at home he started up a howl like a calliope and fastened himself as tight as a leech to Bill's leg. His father peeled him away gradually, like a porous plaster.

94 "How long can you hold him?" asks Bill.

95 "I'm not as strong as I used to be," says old Dorset, "but I think I can promise you ten minutes."

96 "Enough," says Bill. "In ten minutes I shall cross the Central, Southern and Middle Western States, and be legging it trippingly for the Canadian border."

97 And, as dark as it was, and as fat as Bill was, and as good a runner as I am, he was a good mile and a half out of Summit before I could catch up with him.

THINK QUESTIONS

CA-CCSS: CA.RL.7.1, CA.RL.7.4, CA.L.7.4a, CA.L.7.4b, CA.L.7.4d

1. Why do the narrator Sam and his friend Bill Driscoll decide to kidnap the child of Ebenezer Dorset? Cite specific evidence from paragraphs 3 and 4 in your answer.

2. Use details from the text to describe the kidnapped child who comes to be known as Red Chief—based both on stated character traits and on those you infer from details in the text.

3. In his letter, how does Ebenezer Dorset respond to the kidnappers' request for ransom? Draw an inference from the text to explain why he responds in this way. Support your answer with textual evidence.

4. Use context to determine the meaning of the word **acceded** as it is used in paragraph 49 in "The Ransom of Red Chief." Write your definition of *acceded* and tell how you inferred the word's meaning. Then check your inferred meaning in a dictionary to see if it is correct.

5. Remembering that the Greek combining form *phil-* means "loving" and that the base word *progeny* means "children," use the context clues provided in paragraph 3 to determine the meaning of **philoprogenitiveness.** Write your definition of *philoprogenitiveness* and tell how you determined the meaning of this very long word.

CLOSE READ

CA-CCSS: CA.RL.7.1, CA.RL.7.2, CA.RL.7.3, CA.RL.7.4, CA.RL.7.6, CA.L.7.3, CA.W.7.2a, CA.W.7.2b, CA.W.7.2c, CA.W.7.2d, CA.W.7.2e, CA.W.7.2f, CA.W.7.4, CA.W.7.5, CA.W.7.6, CA.W.7.9a, CA.W.7.10

Reread the story "The Ransom of Red Chief." As you reread, complete the Focus Questions below. Then use your answers and annotations from the questions to help you complete the Writing Prompt.

FOCUS QUESTIONS

1. Situational irony occurs when the outcome of a situation contrasts with what was expected to happen. How does the narrator use repetition in paragraphs 1, 3, and 4 to alert readers to the possibility of situational irony? Highlight textual evidence and make annotations to explain your analysis.

2. In paragraphs 1 and 2, explain how the narrator's use of dialect and descriptive language serves to characterize his point of view. Support your response with textual evidence and make annotations to explain your analysis.

3. In paragraph 29, how does the setting suggest that the plot will not proceed as Sam and Bill have anticipated? Highlight textual evidence and make annotations to explain your response.

4. In Sam and Bill's letter to Ebenezer Dorset, they sign "TWO DESPERATE MEN." In what way are these characters desperate as the story begins? How does their sense of desperation change as the plot progresses? Highlight textual evidence and make annotations to support your explanation.

5. In what ways are Sam and Bill challenged by their interactions with Ebenezer Dorset and his son? What do Sam and Bill learn as a result of these interactions? Highlight textual evidence and make annotations to explain your inferences.

WRITING PROMPT

The elements of a story do not exist in isolation. Characters, setting, and plot interact to influence conflict and theme. In "The Ransom of Red Chief," how do the characters, setting, and plot interact to shape the development of the story? Begin with a clear thesis statement to introduce your topic. Use your understanding of story elements, point of view, and inferences to analyze the story. Organize and support your writing with textual evidence, using precise language and selection vocabulary. Include transitions to show the relationships among your ideas, and use a formal style of writing. Provide a conclusion that summarizes your main ideas.

ORANGES

POETRY

Gary Soto

1995

INTRODUCTION

Gary Soto is an award-winning Mexican-American author of poetry, children's books, memoirs, and plays whose work is largely inspired by his experiences growing up among migrant farmworkers in California's Central Valley. Of his poetry, author Joyce Carol Oates has said, "Gary Soto's poems are fast, funny, heartening, and achingly believable, like Polaroid love letters, or snatches of music heard out of a passing car; patches of beauty like patches of sunlight; the very pulse of a life." The poem here, "Oranges," reflects on the emotions of first love

"I fingered
A nickel in my pocket..."

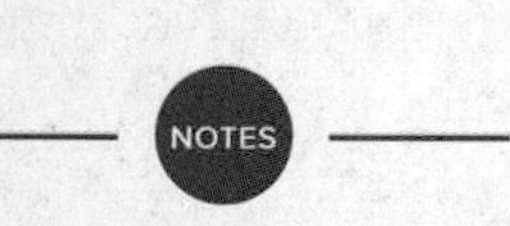

FIRST READ

Oranges

1 The first time I walked
2 With a girl, I was twelve,
3 Cold, and **weighted** down
4 With two oranges in my jacket.
5 December. Frost cracking
6 Beneath my steps, my breath
7 Before me, then gone,
8 As I walked toward
9 Her house, the one whose
10 Porch light burned yellow
11 Night and day, in any weather.
12 A dog barked at me, until
13 She came out pulling
14 At her gloves, face bright
15 With **rouge.** I smiled,
16 Touched her shoulder, and led
17 Her down the street, across
18 A used car lot and a line
19 Of newly planted trees,
20 Until we were breathing
21 Before a drugstore. We
22 Entered, the tiny bell
23 Bringing a saleslady
24 Down a narrow aisle of goods.
25 I turned to the candies
26 **Tiered** like **bleachers,**
27 And asked what she wanted—

28 Light in her eyes, a smile
29 Starting at the corners
30 Of her mouth. I fingered
31 A nickel in my pocket,
32 And when she lifted a chocolate
33 That cost a dime,
34 I didn't say anything.
35 I took the nickel from
36 My pocket, then an orange,
37 And set them quietly on
38 The counter. When I looked up,
39 The lady's eyes met mine,
40 And held them, knowing
41 Very well what it was all
42 About.

43 Outside,
44 A few cars **hissing** past,
45 Fog hanging like old
46 Coats between the trees.
47 I took my girl's hand
48 In mine for two blocks,
49 Then released it to let
50 Her unwrap the chocolate.
51 I peeled my orange
52 That was so bright against
53 The gray of December
54 That, from some distance,
55 Someone might have thought
56 I was making a fire in my hands.

THINK QUESTIONS CA-CCSS: CA.RL.7.1, CA.L.7.4a, CA.L.7.5b, CA.L.7.4c

1. What do you learn about the speaker, his actions, and the setting in lines 1–11? Cite evidence from the text to support your answer.

2. What happens between the boy and the saleswoman in the drugstore? What does the boy's decision to barter suggest about him? Cite textual evidence to support your response.

3. What happens to the two oranges from line 4 that the speaker had in his jacket? Cite evidence from the poem to support your answer.

4. What does the word **weighted** mean as it is used in the phrase *weighted down* in line 3 of the poem? Use the context clues in lines 3–4 to define the meaning of the word. Write your definition of *weighted* and tell how you figured out the word's meaning.

5. What is the meaning of the word **bleachers** in line 26 of the poem? Use context clues to try to figure out the meaning of *bleachers* as it is used in the simile "Tiered like bleachers." How does the analogy of the candies arranged "like bleachers" help you visualize the meaning of the word? Write your definition of *bleachers* and cite the clues you used in the text to help you determine the word's meaning. Then clarify the precise meaning of the word in a print or digital dictionary.

CLOSE READ

CA-CCSS: CA.RL.7.1, CA.RL.7.2, CA.RL.7.4, CA.W.7.2a, CA.W.7.2b, CA.W.7.2c, CA.W.7.2d, CA.W.7.2e, CA.W.7.2f, CA.W.7.4, CA.W.7.5, CA.W.7.6, CA.W.7.9a, CA.W.7.10

Reread the poem "Oranges." As you reread, complete the Focus Questions below. Then use your answers and annotations from the questions to help you complete the Writing Prompt.

FOCUS QUESTIONS

1. Reread and highlight lines 3–6: "Cold, and weighted down / With two oranges in my jacket. / December. Frost cracking / Beneath my steps . . . ." What image do these lines of the poem create in your mind? Which two of the five senses does the image of "Frost cracking / Beneath my steps" appeal to? Cite specific evidence from the text. Make annotations to record your response.

2. Highlight an example of alliteration in lines 20–23. Why do you think the poet uses alliteration in these lines? What does the use of this poetic element add to the poem? Cite specific evidence from the text. Make annotations to explain your response.

3. Highlight an example of onomatopoeia in lines 43–50. What effect does the use of onomatopoeia have on the mood in these lines of the poem? Make annotations to record specific textual evidence to support your answer.

4. Highlight the analogy (or comparison) the speaker is making in lines 51–56. To what is he comparing the orange he is holding? Why does the orange appear so bright? With what is it being contrasted? Make annotations to explain your analysis.

5. What is the theme of the poem? How does the theme illustrate the challenges of human interactions? Highlight examples of human interactions in the poem. Then make annotations to record your answer. Cite specific evidence from the text as support.

WRITING PROMPT

How do the poetic elements in “Oranges” contribute to both the theme and the emotional impact of the poem? Use the details you have compiled from examining the poem to:

- identify how Gary Soto uses figurative language (similes, metaphors, and onomatopoeia) and alliteration to add a deeper level of meaning to the poem
- identify how the use of figurative language creates strong imagery in the poem
- identify how the poetic elements contribute to your understanding of the theme.

Begin with a clear thesis statement to introduce your topic. Remember to organize and to support your writing with specific textual evidence and inferences, using precise language and selection vocabulary. Include transitions to show the relationships among your ideas, and use a formal style of writing. Provide a conclusion that summarizes your key points or ideas.

THE OTHERS

English Language Development

FICTION

INTRODUCTION

Ace and the Jeans gang seem to spend a lot of time in detention, while members of the Well-Offs are enjoying things like after-school tennis lessons. On the way home one afternoon, Ace and Jonboy discover a viciously beaten Jeans member laying in the bushes. Was a Well-Off to blame? Are they all bad people?

"Those were the rich kids with no problems, no responsibilities, and no detentions, ever."

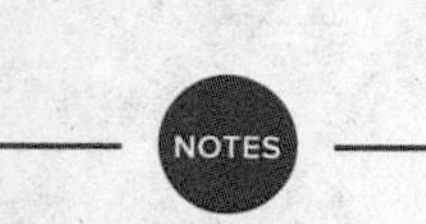

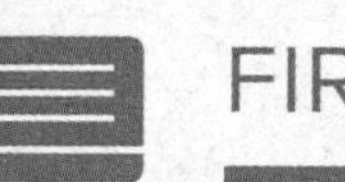

FIRST READ

1 I heard Jonboy's sigh of relief as the school doors whooshed shut behind us. We had been in detention so many times. I couldn't remember what we did this time. All the Jeans boys got detention. The teachers seemed to prefer the fancy Well-Offs. Those were the rich kids with no problems, no responsibilities, and no detentions, ever. Today Mr. Wilson ran detention. He would have made a great prison guard. He hated the Jeans.

2 As we loped toward the park, I noticed Madison and Brittany leaving school. They held their tennis racquets casually. They looked like **expensive** fly swatters. They had special lessons after school. We got detention. I didn't pay much attention to the Well-Off girls. They ignored us. We were too low class. The arrangement was perfect.

3 We headed down the park path. Mom would be mad because of the detention. She wanted me to "better myself." I didn't feel **inferior**. Suddenly I heard Jonboy sort of gurgle and gasp. Brad was sprawled half in the bushes. He wasn't moving. His shirt and jeans were soaked in blood. We pulled him out onto the grass. I could see he had been badly beaten. His face was bleeding in a hundred places. He had a deep cut on his jaw.

4 "Is he dead?" Jonboy croaked.

5 I touched Brad's arm and he groaned. With an inward sigh of relief, I looked at Jonboy. "I know who did this," I muttered. "It was Jason." He threatened Brad before. He called Brad a lowlife. He said Brad was "looking at" Tiffany, Jason's girl. Brad could have stared at Tiffany for hours. She would never have noticed. She was always busy looking in her mirror. Furthermore, Jason's dad was an attorney. He had connections in town. Any trouble Jason got into was quickly smoothed out and forgotten.

6 "What happened?" Madison whimpered. For a **brief** moment I thought Madison would burst into tears. Brittany stood frozen in horror.

NOTES

7 "Who would do anything like this?"

8 "Jason did this, the arrogant Well-Off scum," I **asserted**.

9 "We are not all like Jason," Madison insisted. "Most of us are nice people. We just happened to be born into families that don't worry about money."

10 "Yeah, right," I growled.

11 "Are all you Jeans like Big Bubba?" she demanded. "I bet he has beaten up people who didn't deserve it."

12 It was true. Big Bubba was a **ferocious** fighter. He could knock someone down with one blow of his massive fist.

13 Madison now just looked sad. "We have problems, too. Money doesn't buy happiness. It doesn't guarantee personal peace." She looked at me. "Life is hard, Ace, no matter who you are."

USING LANGUAGE

CA-CCSS: ELD.PII.7.1.Ex

Read each sentence. Choose which of the boldfaced words is a transition word that shows time.

1. The school doors whooshed shut **behind** us **as** we walked **out** of our school.

   ○ behind ○ as ○ out

2. We **were** feeling happy that we could **finally** go **home**.

   ○ were ○ finally ○ home

3. **Before** we left **school**, we had been **in** detention.

   ○ Before ○ school ○ in

4. **Today** Mr. Wilson ran **detention**, which was full of students who had gotten **into** trouble.

   ○ Today ○ detention ○ into

5. **Unlike** us, they had **special** lessons **after** school

   ○ Unlike ○ special ○ after

MEANINGFUL INTERACTIONS CA-CCSS: ELD.PI.7.11.b.Ex

Complete the writing frames below and use the completed sentences to help you participate in the discussion. Then use the self-assessment rubric to evaluate your participation in the discussion.

1. When I express an opinion, I need to ____________________ it with ____________________ ____.

2. I can express my ____________________ with words like *may, possibly, likely,* ____________________, ____________________, and ____________________.

3. An example from "The Others" that I could have an opinion on is how the Jeans and Well-Offs should be treated ____.

4. I can support this opinion with the fact that the Jeans always get ____________________ while the ____.
   This treatment is not ____.

5. Another opinion I have about "The Others" is that ____________________ ____.

6. I can support this opinion by ____________________ ____.

SELF-ASSESSMENT RUBRIC CA-CCSS: ELD.PI.7.11.b.Ex

	4 I did this well.	3 I did this pretty well.	2 I did this a little bit.	1 I did not do this.
I took an active part with others in doing the assigned task.				
I contributed effectively to the group discussion.				
I offered opinions about the text.				
I supported my opinions with evidence from the text.				
I completed the sentences carefully and accurately.				

REREAD

Reread paragraphs 1 through 4 of "The Others." After you reread, complete the Using Language and Meaningful Interactions activities.

USING LANGUAGE

CA-CCSS: ELD.PII.7.2.a.Ex

Read each sentence pair. Complete the chart by writing the noun or plural noun that the boldfaced pronoun refers to.

Question	Noun(s) being referred to
I noticed Madison and Brittany leaving school. **They** were holding their tennis racquets.	
I usually ignored the Well-Off girls. **They** ignored us.	
Brad was lying half in the bushes. **His** clothes were soaked in blood.	
I touched Brad's arm. **He** groaned.	
Big Bubba was a ferocious fighter. **He** could knock someone down with one blow of his massive fist.	

MEANINGFUL INTERACTIONS CA-CCSS: ELD.PI.7.6.a.Ex

The text "The Others" is about two groups of students who go to the same school, but come from different backgrounds and are treated differently. Use the compare-and-contrast chart to help you think of ways the two groups are similar and different. Then use the speaking frames to help you discuss the two groups with your partner. Remember to use evidence from the text to support your comparisons. Use the self-assessment rubric to evaluate your participation in the discussion.

The Jeans	Both	The Well-Offs

- The two groups of students in "The Others" are called . . .
- The . . . seem to like the . . . better than they like the . . .
- I know this because the Jeans . . . but the . . .
- Also, the . . . have more opportunities than . . .
- I know this because . . .
- The . . . and the . . . are not very different because . . .
- Also, some . . . in both groups are . . . , and some are . . .

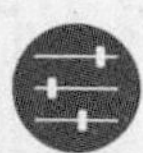

SELF-ASSESSMENT RUBRIC CA-CCSS: ELD.PI.7.6.a.Ex

	4 I did this well.	3 I did this pretty well.	2 I did this a little bit.	1 I did not do this.
I compared and contrasted the two groups of students in the text.				
I listened carefully to my partner's opinions about the text.				
I spoke respectfully when disagreeing with my partner.				
I was courteous when persuading my partner to share my opinion.				

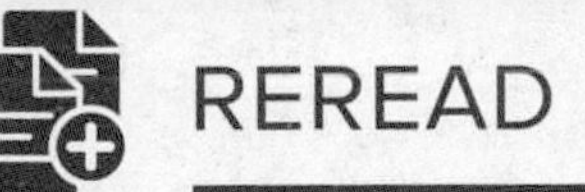

REREAD

Reread paragraphs 5 through 13 of "The Others." After you reread, complete the Using Language and Meaningful Interactions activities.

USING LANGUAGE CA-CCSS: ELD.PII.7.4.Ex

Read each sentence and select what is described by the bolded noun phrase.

1. I heard **Jonboy's sigh of relief** as the school doors whooshed shut behind us.
   - ○ what Jonboy was saying
   - ○ what Jonboy was feeling
   - ○ what kind of doors the school had

2. They looked like **expensive flyswatters**.
   - ○ what the flyswatter was like
   - ○ what the flyswatters were used for
   - ○ when they saw the flyswatters

3. He had a **deep cut** on his jaw.
   - ○ where the cut was
   - ○ when he got the cut
   - ○ what the cut was like

4. Most of us are **nice people**.
   - ○ how many people there are
   - ○ what the people are like
   - ○ where the people are

5. Big Bubba was a **ferocious fighter**.
   - ○ what type of fighter Bubba was
   - ○ who Bubba fights
   - ○ when Bubba fights

MEANINGFUL INTERACTIONS CA-CCSS: ELD.PI.7.6.a.Ex

With your partner, decide who will present how the Well-Offs and the Jeans are similar and who will present how they are different. Use the writing frames below to help you present. Practice presenting to your partner.

Partner 1

The Well-Offs and the Jeans have some things in common.

They are similar because both ______________________________.

I know this is true because ______________________________
______________________________.

Partner 2

The Well-Offs and the Jeans are different in some ways.

They are different because ______________________________
______________________________.

I know this is true because ______________________________
______________________________.

DEEP WATER

English Language Development

FICTION

INTRODUCTION

For best friends Elizabeth and Sophie, swimming is the most important part of their lives. For years, they trained together, working hard to reach their goals. Now, at age 17, they both want the only spot available on a top swim team. How will they prepare for the competition? Who will be good enough to make the team?

"At last, they were to compete in the most important swim meet of their lives."

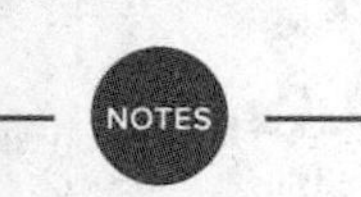

FIRST READ

1 Elizabeth and Sophie shared everything, especially their **enthusiasm** for swimming. At age 17, their identities began and ended with the word "swimmer." The girls competed with each other, their teammates, and their personal best times.

2 When they first began swimming, Elizabeth was the faster swimmer. Sophie had to struggle to keep up. She worked extraordinarily hard. She trained long hours to improve her **performance**. Elizabeth was as fierce as a coach. She helped with demanding workouts. They spent hours lifting weights and doing aerobic training. They swam at least eight miles a week. Each tried to outdo the other. Their competition, focus, and determination increased. Both dreamed of being on Team USA, the swim team that competed internationally.

3 At last, they were to compete in the most important swim meet of their lives. The winner would qualify for Team USA. Only one **slot** was available, so only one girl would make the team. The other competitors would not.

4 Two weeks before the event, Elizabeth stood on the edge of the pool. Sophie was finishing her final training lap. A distance had been growing between them.

5 "We need to talk," Elizabeth declared.

6 "It's about the meet, right?" Sophie said. "We worked hard, and we trained together. Now, it's not about us anymore. It's about me. It's about you. It's about winning the meet."

7 "I think it's best if we just train separately," Elizabeth stated. "It's the only way."

NOTES

8 The girls chose different times for endurance training and weightlifting. Although time in the pool **inevitably** overlapped, they swam in widely separated lanes.

9 Elizabeth and Sophie made it to the finals along with Bethany, another member of their team. They would be swimming in the individual medley, which consisted of the four competitive swimming strokes.

10 The girls pushed off the side of the pool. They glided sleekly through the water. Elizabeth was vaguely aware of Sophie and Bethany, but her entire focus was on moving through the water as effortlessly as a shark. She **propelled** herself 15 meters before surfacing.

11 Sophie knew that the butterfly was her best swim stroke. Her muscles flexed and moved smoothly.

12 In the last lap, muscles screaming, each girl pushed herself to reach the other side of the pool. When they surfaced, the roar of the crowd was deafening. The judges wanted to see the video of the finish to determine who touched the side with her hand first. Elizabeth and Sophie looked at each other and clambered out of the pool. They hugged and then headed for the locker room. They left before the announcement.

13 "Ladies and gentlemen, the winner of the individual medley and new member of Team USA is..."

USING LANGUAGE

CA-CCSS: ELD.PI.7.12.b.Ex, ELD.PI.7.12.b.Ex

Complete both charts below by filling in the correct answers to the third and fourth columns from the options.

Add Prefix *inter-* Options	New Meaning Options
interact interstate	dealings across more than one political territory acting in a way that affects others

Word	Meaning	Add Prefix *inter-*	New Meaning
state (noun)	a political territory of a government		
act (verb)	behave		

Add Suffix *-tion* or *-ly* Options		New Meaning Options
qualification smoothly widely	vaguely determination	something you need in order to do something something done in an even way a strong desire to do something something done in an unclear way something done in a wide way

Word	Meaning	Add Suffix *-tion* or *-ly*	New Meaning
determine (verb)	to decide		
qualify (verb)	to be allowed to do something		
wide (adjective)	a large side-to-side measurement		
smooth (adjective)	even		
vague (adjective)	unclear		

MEANINGFUL INTERACTIONS CA-CCSS: ELD.PI.7.12.a.Ex

Work with your partner to discuss figurative language in "Deep Water." Use the speaking frames below to help guide your discussion. Then use the self-assessment rubric to evaluate your participation in the discussion.

Paragraph 10 includes the simile "Her focus was on **moving through the water as effortlessly as a shark.**"

- The phrase "moving through the water as effortlessly as a shark" is a simile because . . .
- The simile means . . .
- Another way to say this is " . . . "
- The simile helps the reader "see" . . .

Paragraph 12 includes personification in the sentence "In the last lap, **muscles screaming,** each girl pushed herself to reach the other side of the pool."

- The phrase "muscles screaming" is an example of personification because . . .
- The personification helps the reader . . .

SELF-ASSESSMENT RUBRIC CA-CCSS: ELD.PI.7.1.Ex

	4 I did this well.	3 I did this pretty well.	2 I did this a little bit.	1 I did not do this.
I took an active part with my partner in doing the assigned task.				
I contributed effectively to our decisions.				
I understood the use of figurative language in the selection.				
I helped my partner understand the use of figurative language in the selection.				
I completed the sentences about figurative language carefully and accurately.				

REREAD

Reread paragraphs 1 through 6 of "Deep Water." After you reread, complete the Using Language and Meaningful Interactions activities.

USING LANGUAGE CA-CCSS: ELD.PII.7.5.Ex

An adverb or adverbial phrase modifies, or gives information about, an adjective or verb. It tells how, when, where, or why something happened.

Complete each sentence by writing an adverb or adverbial phrase in the blank. Use information from the text "Deep Water."

1. **Write an adverbial phrase in the following sentence.**

   At last, the girls were to compete ________________________________.

2. **Write an adverbial phrase in the following sentence.**

   The winner would qualify ________________________________.

3. **Write an adverb in the following sentence.**

   We worked hard and we trained ________________________________.

4. **Write an adverbial phrase in the following sentence.**

   They swam ________________________________.

5. **Write an adverb in the following sentence.**

   Sophie's muscles flexed and moved________________________________.

6. **Write an adverbial phrase in the following sentence.**

   Sophie and Elizabeth's friendship grew ________________________________.

7. **Write an adverb in the following sentence.**

   An expert swimmer trains ________________________________.

MEANINGFUL INTERACTIONS CA-CCSS: ELD.PI.7.6.c.Ex, ELD.PI.7.12.a.Ex

The author of "Deep Water" uses specific words to describe events. Read the following sentences with your group. Discuss how the boldfaced word helps convey the meaning of the sentence. Then replace each boldfaced word with a synonym and an antonym. Discuss with your group how the meaning of the sentence has changed. Use the self-assessment rubric to evaluate your participation in the discussion.

Both girls **dreamed** of being on Team USA.

- Synonym: ____________ Both girls ____________ on Team USA.

  The synonym changes the sentence a lot / a little because . . .

- Antonym: ____________ Both girls ____________ on Team USA.

  The antonym changes the sentence a lot / a little because . . .

Elizabeth moved through the water **effortlessly**.

- Synonym: ____________ Elizabeth moved through the water ____________.

  The synonym changes the sentence a lot / a little because . . .

- Antonym: ____________ Elizabeth moved through the water ____________.

  The antonym changes the sentence a lot / a little because . . .

SELF-ASSESSMENT RUBRIC CA-CCSS: ELD.PI.7.11.b.Ex

	4 I did this well.	3 I did this pretty well.	2 I did this a little bit.	1 I did not do this.
I expressed my ideas about the synonyms and antonyms clearly.				
I listened carefully to others' ideas about synonyms and antonyms.				
I spoke respectfully when disagreeing with my group members.				
I was courteous when persuading my group members to share my opinion about synonyms and antonyms.				

REREAD

Reread paragraphs 7 through 12 of "Deep Water." After you reread, complete the Using Language and Meaningful Interactions activities.

USING LANGUAGE CA-CCSS: ELD.PII.7.7.Ex

Complete the sentences by filling in the blanks.

1. **What three ideas make up the sentence "The girls competed with each other, their teammates, and their personal best times"?**

   The girls competed ____________________. The girls competed ____________________.

   The girls competed ____.

2. **What three ideas make up the sentence "Their competition, focus, and determination increased"?**

   Their ____________________________. Their ____________________________.

   Their ____________________________.

3. **What two ideas make up the sentence "Both dreamed of being on Team USA, the swim team that competed internationally"?**

   Both dreamed ____.

   Team USA is ____.

4. **Write these separate ideas as one condensed sentence: "We worked hard. We trained together."**

   We __________________________, and ____________________________.

5. **Write these separate ideas as one condensed sentence: "The girls surfaced. The roar of the crowd was deafening."**

   When __________________________, the ____________________________.

6. **Write these separate ideas as one condensed sentence: "Elizabeth and Sophie hugged. Then they headed for the locker room."**

   Elizabeth and Sophie ____________, and __________________________________.

MEANINGFUL INTERACTIONS CA-CCSS: ELD.PI.7.6.c.Ex, ELD.PI.7.12.a.Ex

You will continue your discussion on synonyms and how they affect a sentence's meaning. With your group, decide which sentence to present and circle the sentence below. Complete the sentence of your choice with a synonym that you used in the previous discussion.

- Both girls ________________________________ of being on Team USA.
- Elizabeth moved through the water ________________________________.

________________________ is a synonym for ________________________.

Then use a dictionary to find the meaning of the synonym. Discuss with your group how changing to the synonym affects the sentence. Use the writing frames below to record your thoughts and be prepared to present your ideas to the class.

In this sentence, the word means ________________________________.

It affects the sentence ________________________________

____

____.

EXTENDED WRITING PROJECT

74%

2:40 PM

app.studysync.com

ASSIGNMENTS REVIEW BINDER BLASTS LIBRARY

studysync®

WRITE

Extended Writing Project Prompt and Directions:

As you've seen in the short stories and novel and play e[illegible] interactions are often complicated. Sometimes, we're u[illegible] actions not only with other humans but also with the en[illegible] should we do about the "invasive alien species" (sounds [illegible] we've introduced into California—species that are threat[illegible] animals? It's your call. Write an argumentative essay in wh[illegible] caused by human interaction (interference) with the environm[illegible] Invasive Plant Inventory" to review the issue of invasive species. [illegible] an invasive plant or animal, such as the Burmese python that people have [illegible] the Florida Everglades or kudzu, a spreading invasive plant. Research your invasive plant or animal in at least three print or digital sources, such as books, magazines, or reliable websites. As you research, ask yourself: Should humans try to solve this problem or let nature take its course?

Your argument should include:

- an explicitly stated claim about whether or not humans should try to clean up the "mess" they started
- persuasive reasons and relevant textual evidence, logically organized
- acknowledgment of opposing claims or other points of view
- citations of your sources in your essay and in a Works Cited page
- a conclusion that restates your claim and summarizes your persuasive evidence

ASSIGNMENT

EXTENDED WRITING PROJECT

ARGUMENTATIVE WRITING

Extended Writing Project: Argumentative Writing by StudySync

1 WRITE

Font Size

The I'm

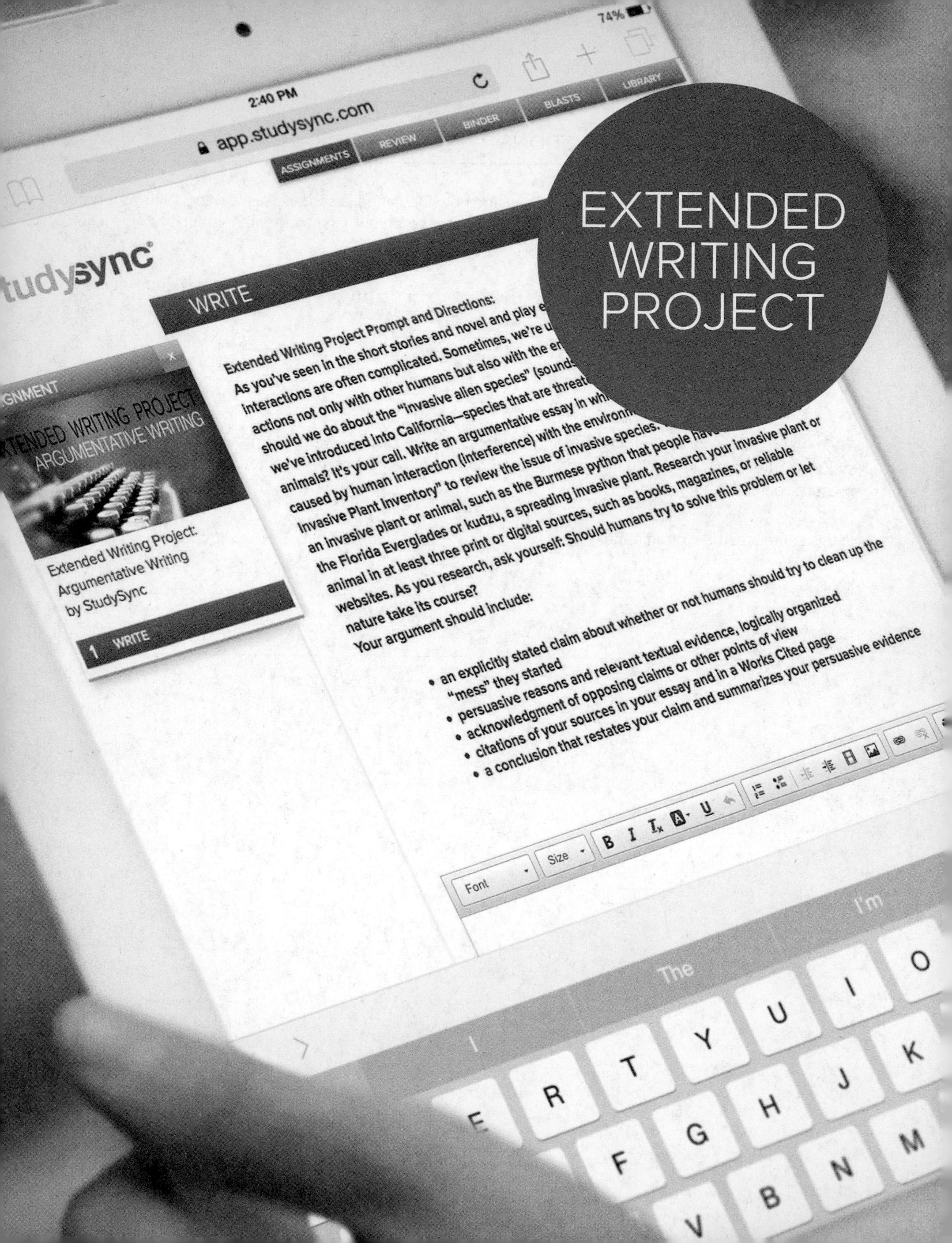

NOTES

ARGUMENTATIVE WRITING

WRITING PROMPT

As you've seen in the short stories and novel and play excerpts in this unit, human interactions are often complicated. Sometimes, we're unaware of the consequences of our actions not only with other humans but also with the environment. For example, what should we do about the "invasive alien species" (sounds like science fiction, doesn't it?) we've introduced into California—species that are threatening the state's native plants and animals? It's your call. Write an argumentative essay in which you explore the challenges caused by human interaction (interference) with the environment. First, reread "California Invasive Plant Inventory" to review the issue of invasive species. Then do research. Choose an invasive plant or animal, such as the Burmese python that people have introduced into the Florida Everglades or kudzu, a spreading invasive plant. Research your invasive plant or animal in at least three print or digital sources, such as books, magazines, or reliable websites. As you research, ask yourself: Should humans try to solve this problem or let nature take its course?

Your argument should include:

- an explicitly stated claim about whether humans should try to clean up the "mess" they started
- persuasive reasons and relevant textual evidence, logically organized
- acknowledgment of opposing claims or other points of view
- citations of your sources in your essay and in a Works Cited page
- a conclusion that restates your claim and summarizes your persuasive evidence

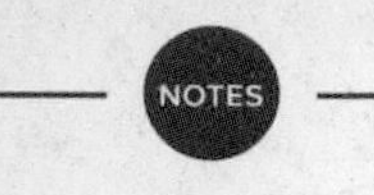

An argumentative essay is a form of persuasive writing. In an argument, the writer makes a claim about a topic and then provides evidence—facts, details, examples, and quotations—to support that claim. After explicitly stating the claim in the opening section of the essay, the writer develops his or her ideas with a specific audience in mind and presents the evidence in the body of the argument, using transitions to link related ideas. The purpose of the argument is to convince readers to accept and agree with the writer's claim.

In order to provide convincing supporting evidence for an argumentative essay, the writer must often do outside research, either because it is assigned or because it is essential to understanding a complex topic. That means the writer must look at print or digital sources of information related to the topic—books, articles, Web pages, blogs, diaries, letters, interviews, and other documents, and incorporate the information that he or she finds into the argument. The writer cites the sources of the evidence that he or she presents in the body of the essay so that readers will know where it came from. (In other Extended Writing Project Lessons, you will learn more about how to select appropriate source material, incorporate your research, and cite your sources.)

The features of an argumentative essay include the following:

- an introduction that states a claim about the topic
- a clearly organized presentation of logical reasoning and relevant evidence
- embedded quotations from credible sources that are clearly cited
- acknowledgment of alternate or opposing claims
- language that clarifies the relationship between the claim and the reasons that support it
- a concluding statement that follows from the argument

As you continue working on this extended writing project, you'll learn more about crafting each of the elements of an argumentative essay with research.

STUDENT MODEL

Before you get started, read this argumentative essay that one student wrote in response to the writing prompt. As you read this Student Model, highlight and annotate the features of an argumentative essay that the student included.

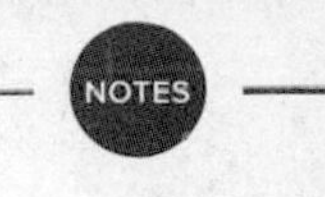

What Do We Do About Invasive Alien Species?

How many science-fiction movies have you seen about alien invasions from Mars or elsewhere and the effects that these alien invaders have had on the people and places on Earth? But as the saying goes, truth is often stranger than fiction, and today, humans are facing a real alien invasion, except this time the invaders are not extraterrestrials in the usual sense. They are invasive alien plants and animals that humans have thoughtlessly introduced into areas where they do not belong. What is the effect of this harmful human activity? Nothing less than the extinction of many of the world's native wildlife! But what can be done about this growing problem? Should humans be forced to clean up the mess they started? Or should humans do nothing and let nature take its course? These are the two sides to the issue. This essay will argue that humans need to take action to solve the problem of invasive species before it's too late to save our native wildlife. The question is, how? But first, let's look at the issue.

According to a recent online article, "Invasive Species," published by the National Wildlife Federation, "Approximately, 42% of Threatened or Endangered species are at risk primarily due to invasive species" ("Invasive Species" 1). But what is an invasive species, and why does it pose such a threat to native plants and animals? An invasive non-native species is one that enters a new ecosystem and then settles and reproduces so successfully that it threatens the existence of the area's native species and the balance of the ecosystem itself ("Invasive Species" 1). These invaders, which may not have any natural predators in the new ecosystem, take over an area, destroying the native wildlife that probably have no defenses against them.

Unfortunately, many examples of alien species invasions exist today across the United States. According to the research report in this unit, "California Invasive Plant Inventory," approximately 200 non-native invasive plant species are threatening the state's wildlands—"public and private lands that support native ecosystems"— and these plants can "displace native species" and even "alter ecosystem[s]" ("CIPI" 2). Although these invasive plant species pose a danger to California's wildlands, perhaps no greater threat by an invasive species exists today than that of the Burmese python in the Florida Everglades.

In her article "Snakes on the 'Glades," published online in *U.S. News & World Report,* Laura Bradley explains that "the Burmese python first arrived in Florida

as part of the exotic pet trade, and over time made its way into the Everglades as overwhelmed pet owners released the animals into the wild or they escaped" (Bradley 2). As a result of the actions of these irresponsible pet owners, Florida is facing a huge problem today. According to Michael Sarill, in his blog "Burmese Pythons in the Everglades," scientists estimate that "anywhere between 30,000 and 150,000 Burmese Pythons exist in South Florida" (Sarill 1). Because pythons are good at hiding, scientists do not know how many are really out there. Yet according to Sarill, they do know that the population of native species has declined 90 percent in recent years—including 100 percent for rabbits and some other small mammals (Sarill 1). Think of the effects of this over time: The pythons could cause the extinction of every native animal species in the Everglades. Even the alligators are not safe. Pythons have been known to take on alligators and win (Sarill 3)!

But what can be done? After the death of a two-year-old child by one of these pythons, humans began taking steps to slow the growth and spread of these non-native reptiles (Sarill 4). However, some people wonder if this approach is correct or even possible. They say that nature should just take its course. We should do nothing because this is a perfect example of the "survival of the fittest"--the idea that the strongest will survive. Another argument by advocates for doing nothing about the problem is that once the pythons have eaten all the small animals, they might turn on themselves. But if that happens, only the biggest and strongest pythons will survive. Would any human be safe?

There are a couple of flaws in the do-nothing argument. First, it shows a lack of responsibility. People caused the invasion of the Burmese python, so they should do something about it. In addition, nobody knows what might happen when the python has eaten all the animals in the area. Sarill worries that rural communities might be in danger. He states, "As food sources run out, the snakes will grow increasingly desperate in search of a new meal. If a snake is willing to attack a large alligator, household pets are unquestionably vulnerable to attack" (Sarill 4). The problem is really complicated, and given the impact on the environment by invasive species (which were introduced by humans in the first place), we humans really must try to restore nature's balance.

Despite the difficulties, the only way to solve the problem is to remove the pythons from the Everglades. In recent years, Florida has held month-long python hunts.

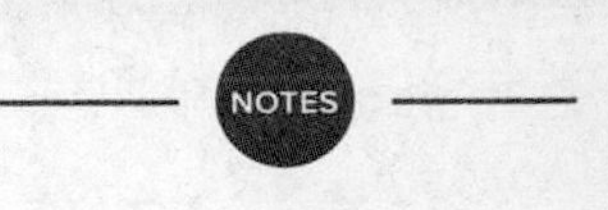

People came from around the nation to hunt the snakes in 2012, but only 68 were collected (Bradley 3). Although that hunt didn't destroy many pythons, researchers did gather important information about where and how the snakes live, which can help them develop other strategies, but these solutions are far into the future.

In the meantime, the problem of invasive alien species is growing—both ecologically and economically. According to Bradley, the nation "spends more than $120 billion each year dealing with 50,000 introduced species of plants, animals, and microbes" (Bradley 1-2). If we can't control 18-foot-long, 200-pound pythons, how can we even begin to fight against thousands of microbes? Yet we must try, and we must be part of the solution. We humans have had both a positive and negative impact on our environment. When we make a mistake, such as releasing a dangerous predator like the Burmese python into the wild, we must do everything we can to make things right.

Works Cited

Bradley, Laura. "Snakes on the 'Glades." *U.S. News & World Report* 21 July 2014. Web. 9 Dec. 2014. <http://www.usnews.com/news/articles/2014/07/21/invasive-pythons-threaten-florida-everglades>

California Invasive Plant Council. "California Invasive Plant Inventory." 2006. Print.

"Invasive Species." National Wildlife Federation. Web. 9 Dec. 2014 <http:// www.nwf.org/wildlife/threats-to-wildlife/invasive-species.aspx>

Sarill, Michael. "Burmese Pythons in the Everglades." *Baboon* 12 Sept. 2013. Web. 9 Dec. 2014. <http://www.baboongame.com/blog/burmese-pythons-everglades#.VIc9NVrgA1Q>

THINK QUESTIONS

1. The writer of the Student Model states an opinion (or claim) about whether humans should take action to solve the problem of invasive species. What is the writer's opinion (or claim)? How does the writer support it? What reasons does he or she give? Cite specific evidence from the Student Model in your response.

2. What relevant evidence did the writer include in the Student Model to support his or her opinion (or claim)? Cite the evidence and explain why it is relevant.

3. Write two or three sentences evaluating the writer's conclusion. Cite specific textual evidence from the last paragraph.

4. Think about the writing prompt. Which selections, Blasts, or other resources would you like to use or research to write your own argumentative essay? Give strong reasons for your choice.

5. Based on the selections you have read, listened to, or researched, how would you answer the question, "What are the challenges of human interactions?" What are some ideas that you might consider in the argument you'll be developing for your essay?

PREWRITE

CA-CCSS: CA.W.7.1a, CA.W.7.1b, CA.W.7.4, CA.W.7.5, CA.W.7.8, CA.W.7.9b, CA.W.7.10

WRITING PROMPT

As you've seen in the short stories and novel and play excerpts in this unit, human interactions are often complicated. Sometimes, we're unaware of the consequences of our actions not only with other humans but also with the environment. For example, what should we do about the "invasive alien species" (sounds like science fiction, doesn't it?) we've introduced into California—species that are threatening the state's native plants and animals? It's your call. Write an argumentative essay in which you explore the challenges caused by human interaction (interference) with the environment. First, reread "California Invasive Plant Inventory" to review the issue of invasive species. Then do research. Choose an invasive plant or animal, such as the Burmese python that people have introduced into the Florida Everglades or kudzu, a spreading invasive plant. Research your invasive plant or animal in at least three print or digital sources, such as books, magazines, or reliable websites. As you research, ask yourself: Should humans try to solve this problem or let nature take its course?

Your argument should include:

- an explicitly stated claim about whether humans should try to clean up the "mess" they started
- persuasive reasons and relevant textual evidence, logically organized
- acknowledgment of opposing claims or other points of view
- citations of your sources in your essay and in a Works Cited page
- a conclusion that restates your claim and summarizes your persuasive evidence

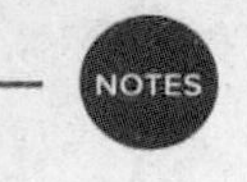

Your first step is to think about the problem of invasive species so that you can decide which side you're on. Are you for removing invasive species, or do you think we should leave them alone? Follow the directions in the prompt by reading "California's Invasive Plant Inventory" to explore what an invasive species is. Then use the prewriting strategies you've learned—list making, brainstorming, free writing, concept mapping, sketching, and so on—to figure out which side of the issue you're on.

Try this: Draw a two-column chart. Label one column "Pro" and the other column "Con." Then fill in each column with your ideas about the benefits of taking action against invasive species ("Pro") versus leaving the species alone ("Con"). In the columns, jot down words and phrases or draw pictures. Now look at your responses. Which side of the argument do you seem to be on? Express your opinion in a complete sentence above your chart, based on what you already know. Here's what the writer of the Student Model wrote: "I think humans should try to control the spread of invasive species because we caused the problem, so it's up to us to fix it."

Needless to say, there are still quite a few questions you need to answer before you can take a stand on the issue. First, choose an invasive species to write about. That may take some research. Next, make a list of research questions. You'll want to ask good research questions that will help you make a strong claim and lead you to strong reasons and evidence that will support your claim. The answers you discover during your research will help you build an effective argument about invasive species and whether we should take action against them.

The writer of the Student Model had a great many questions. He or she used a chart to organize them, to record answers based on what he or she already knew, and to identify sources to research the questions and find the answers.

Topic: Invasive species

Claim: "I think humans should try to control the spread of invasive species because we caused the problem, so it's up to us to fix it."

RESEARCH QUESTIONS	ANSWERS BASED ON WHAT I KNOW NOW	POSSIBLE SOURCES FOR MORE RESEARCH
What is an invasive species?	Invasive species are not native to an area. They take over a place by eating the native species, breeding, and spreading.	Print or online newspaper articles, articles in science magazines or journals, wildlife organizations and newsletters, print or online encyclopedias, radio or TV programs, documentaries, websites, including government websites, and blogs
Which invasive species might I want to learn more about?	My grandmother lives in Florida, so I want to know more about Burmese pythons!	Local newspaper and magazine articles and websites, especially government websites, blogs, wildlife organizations, and newsletters
What causes invasive species to come into an area?	Human activity is a major cause because people let exotic pets escape, or introduce plants or animals into an area where they don't belong.	Newspaper articles, newsletters, articles in science magazines or journals, print or online encyclopedias, documentaries, websites, blogs, radio and TV shows about science or the work of wildlife organizations
What are some problems caused by these invasive species?	Burmese pythons have invaded the Everglades and are eating native species in the area, causing some wildlife to become extinct.	Newspaper articles, articles in science magazines, radio programs, websites, especially government websites, blogs, science TV shows, wildlife organizations, and newsletters

RESEARCH QUESTIONS	ANSWERS BASED ON WHAT I KNOW NOW	POSSIBLE SOURCES FOR MORE RESEARCH
What are some solutions to the problems caused by these invasive species?	Removing the pythons from the Everglades is one solution I've heard about.	Newspaper articles, articles in science magazines, radio programs, websites, especially government web sites, blogs, wildlife organizations
How effective are these solutions?	I don't know. I don't think it's going well because the pythons are still a problem in the Everglades.	Newspaper articles, articles in science magazines, radio or TV programs about science, websites, especially government websites, blogs, wildlife organizations, and newsletters
What would happen if we left invasive species alone? Would that be a good or bad thing?	I think the pythons would eat up every other species. That can't be good!	Newspaper articles, articles in science magazines, radio or TV programs about science, websites, especially government websites, blogs, wildlife organizations, and newsletters

Create a similar graphic organizer on your own. Do some research to answer your questions. Then select an invasive species and take a stand on the issue. You can always change your species or your opinion as you do more research and develop your ideas.

NOTES

SKILL: RESEARCH AND NOTE-TAKING

DEFINE

If you have already completed research presentations for previous units, then you have already learned how to do research. **Research** is how you discover information or double-check facts or ideas. Research can be as simple as scanning social media for current trends, looking up the meaning of an unfamiliar word in a dictionary, tuning in the radio for details about local school closures, going online to learn how to play chess, or trying something new to get firsthand experience.

Unless you have a perfect memory, **note-taking** is essential to effective research. Each time you gather information from a source, you should take notes. A **source** might be a textbook, a newspaper article, a website, an app, an encyclopedia, or an authority on a subject that interests you. Your **notes** should always include the title of the source, its author's name, and the place (print or Web) and date of publication. Once you have that information, you can jot down all the ideas you learned from that source. This might seem like a lot of work, but it's a good practice. For example, you might need to go back later to double-check a fact. Your notes will help save time in finding that source again. You also need this information in order to prepare citations and a Works Cited section at the end of your argumentative essay. Your Works Cited section can help your readers learn more about your topic and ideas. And your readers will be able to use the information about your sources to answer their own questions and do their own research.

Keep your purpose for writing in mind as you do your research. In this unit, you will be writing an argumentative essay. The point of your research is to find facts, details, examples, and quotations that support your claim about why humans should or should not take action against invasive species. Your researched information should help persuade readers to accept your claim and agree with you.

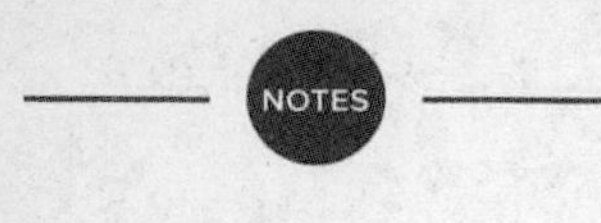

IDENTIFICATION AND APPLICATION

- Before you begin your research, choose a topic. Then do some general reading about it. You might find that the topic doesn't interest you or that you can't find enough evidence to support a claim. If that's the case, choose another topic on which to focus your research.
- Narrow your topic. Some topics are so broad—invasive species around the world, human interactions on Earth—that you could spend years doing research. Try narrowing your topic to one specific aspect—the Burmese pythons in the Everglades, the impact of climbers on Mount Everest— and then look for specific information as you research.
- Ask questions. Remember all those research questions you created in the Prewrite lesson? Keep them in mind as you think about your topic and do your research. As you research, you probably will come up with more questions. That's good. These questions will help you focus your topic even more and determine what you really need to know.
- Use thoughtful key word searches when researching online. Enter specific words and phrases rather than general topics. You will likely have to fine-tune the words and phrases in order to get to accurate and reliable sources.
- Choose your sources carefully. Think about their accuracy and reliability, especially when searching online. Look for well-known sources, such as fact-based newspapers, magazines, and journals. Try to stick to educational and government websites (ending in .edu and .gov instead of .com or .org)—their information is usually more reliable.
- Remember the difference between primary and secondary sources. Primary sources are firsthand accounts written by people who witnessed the events they describe. Autobiographies, diaries, letters, interviews, and memoirs are primary sources. They are good sources for direct quotations. Secondary sources are written after the fact. They combine information from different primary sources. Textbooks, encyclopedia articles, history books, and magazine articles are examples of secondary sources. These are especially good for background information. Go ahead and check *their* sources. They can lead you to helpful primary sources.
- Stay focused when you take notes. Look for the answers to your research questions. Think about your purpose and audience. Don't get distracted by irrelevant information.
- Take careful notes. If you prefer to write your notes on index cards, use one card for each source. Be sure to include the title, author, and publication information on the card. If you need more than one card for the same source, number the cards consecutively. You can also take

notes digitally. Use a word-processing program. Open a new document for each source. At the top of the page, identify the title, author, and publication information. Then write your notes. Use bullets or new paragraphs for each new set of facts. There are also note-taking apps and easy-to-use software.

- If you want to quote from a source, write down the words exactly as they appear in the source and place them within quotation marks. Be sure to give credit to the source in your writing. Sometimes you might want to paraphrase, or restate, the ideas. That's a great way to condense ideas. But you still must cite the original source so that readers know where you found the information.
- Citing your sources is very important. It helps you avoid plagiarizing, or presenting other people's words and ideas as your own. Follow this rule: Anytime you use any information from a researched source, give credit to that source.

MODEL

Consider the following paragraph from the second paragraph of the Student Model, "What Do We Do About Invasive Alien Species?":

> *According to a recent online article, "Invasive Species," published by the National Wildlife Federation,* ***"Approximately, 42% of Threatened or Endangered species are at risk primarily due to invasive species" ("Invasive Species" 1).*** *But what is an invasive species, and why does it pose such a threat to native plants and animals?* ***An invasive non-native species is one that enters a new ecosystem and then settles and reproduces so successfully that it threatens the existence of the area's native species and the balance of the ecosystem itself ("Invasive Species" 1).*** *These invaders, which may not have any natural predators in the new ecosystem, take over an area, destroying the native wildlife that probably have no defenses against them.*

The writer presents his or her research in a couple of different ways. First, the writer uses a direct quotation that he or she thinks is relevant to the ideas in the paragraph. Next, he or she introduces the quoted material by identifying its source—a recent online article called "Invasive Species" that was published by the National Wildlife Federation. Then the writer shows the exact words within quotation marks. After the quoted material, he or she provides a citation in parentheses. Because the article doesn't have a stated author, the writer uses the title and page number on which the quoted material appeared.

The article "Invasive Species" was very helpful to the writer. Later in the paragraph, he or she cites it again. This time, instead of quoting from the source, the writer paraphrases some of the information. This means that the writer uses his or her own words to define what an invasive species is. However, because the definition came from a source, the writer provides a citation.

PRACTICE

Do some research for a quotation about the invasive species you will be writing about in your argumentative essay. Write down the quotation exactly as it appears in the source. Then, for practice, restate the quotation in your own words and cite its source. As always, record the source's title, author, date, and publication information in your notes.

NOTES

SKILL: THESIS STATEMENT

DEFINE

The thesis of an argumentative essay takes the form of a claim. A claim is the writer's opinion about the topic of the essay. It is a statement of position, belief, or judgment. A claim might be introduced with certain phrases that make the writer's point of view clear, such as "I believe," "I think," "We should," or "One must." An opinion cannot be proven to be true, but it can be supported with relevant evidence—facts, statistics, quotations from experts, examples, and so on. The claim of an argument typically appears in the introductory paragraph, often as the last sentence.

IDENTIFICATION AND APPLICATION

A thesis statement, or claim, in an argumentative essay

- explicitly states the writer's opinion about the topic of the essay.
- previews the ideas, reasons, and evidence that will be presented in the body paragraphs of the essay.
- addresses all aspects of the argumentative prompt.
- is stated directly in the introductory paragraph.

MODEL

The following is the introductory paragraph from the Student Model essay "What Do We Do About Invasive Alien Species?":

> *How many science-fiction movies have you seen about alien invasions from Mars or elsewhere and the effects that these alien invaders have had on the people and places on Earth? But as the saying goes, truth is often stranger than fiction, and today, humans are facing a real alien invasion, except this*

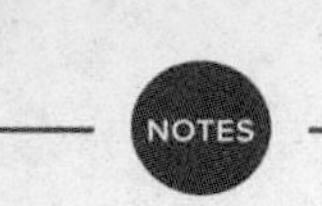

time the invaders are not extraterrestrials in the usual sense. They are invasive alien plants and animals that humans have thoughtlessly introduced into areas where they do not belong. What is the effect of this harmful human activity? Nothing less than the extinction of many of the world's native wildlife! But what can be done about this growing problem? Should humans be forced to clean up the mess they started? Or should humans do nothing and let nature take its course? These are the two sides to the issue. **This essay will argue that humans need to take action to solve the problem before it's too late to save our native wildlife.** The question is, how? But first, let's look at the issue.

Notice the boldfaced claim near the end of the essay's opening paragraph. This student's claim responds to the writing prompt by taking a stand on the issue of invasive species: The writer believes that humans need to solve the problem. Instead of using the words "I think," the writer says, "This essay will argue," but the meaning is the same. The writer believes that human intervention is necessary. Notice how in the sentences following the claim, the writer previews the ideas to be discussed in the body of the paper. He or she will explore the issue of invasive species and then talk about how the problem can be solved through human interaction.

PRACTICE

Write a thesis statement for your argumentative essay. It should explicitly state where you stand on the issue of invasive species. You don't need to identify the specific invasive species you chose as your topic, but you can. After writing your claim, exchange it with a partner. Offer each other feedback. How clear is your partner's claim? Is it obvious where he or she stands on the issue of invasive species? Does the claim address all the parts of the prompt? Offer each other suggestions. Make constructive, supportive comments that will help your partner develop an effective thesis.

NOTES

SKILL: ORGANIZE ARGUMENTATIVE WRITING

DEFINE

As you have learned, the purpose of argumentative writing is to persuade readers to accept the writer's thesis statement, or claim. To do so, the writer must organize and present his or her reasons and relevant evidence—the facts, examples, statistics, and quotations found during research—in a logical and convincing way. The writer must also select an **organizational structure** that best suits the argument.

Writers of arguments can choose from a number of organizational structures, including **compare-contrast, order of importance, problem-solution, cause-effect, and chronological (or sequential) order,** among others. Experienced writers use **transition words and phrases** to help readers understand which organizational structure is being used. As they plan, writers often use an outline or another graphic organizer to determine the most persuasive way to present their ideas and evidence.

Writers are not limited to using only one organizational structure throughout a text. Within a specific section or paragraph, they might use a different organizational structure. This does not affect the overall organization, however.

IDENTIFICATION AND APPLICATION

- When selecting an overall organizational structure for an argument, a writer must consider the claim he or she is making. Then the writer must think about the best way to present the evidence that supports it. Do this by asking these questions:
  - To support my claim, should I compare and contrast ideas or details in the text?
  - Is there an order of importance to my evidence? Is some evidence stronger than other evidence? Or does all my evidence support my idea equally well?

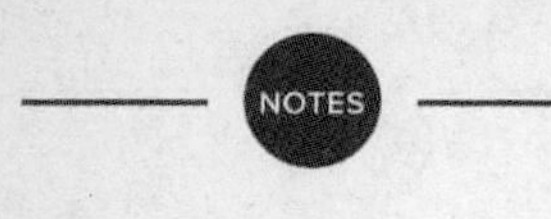

› In my claim, have I identified a problem? Do I have supporting evidence that suggests a solution or an answer?
› Does my supporting evidence suggest a cause or an effect?
› To support my claim, does it make sense to retell an event or a series of events in chronological (or time) order?

- Writers often use signal, or cue, words and phrases to help readers recognize the organizational structure of their writing. These words and phrases are also known as transitions:
  › Compare and contrast: *like, and, both, similarly, in the same way* to compare and *unlike, different from, while, but, however, although, on the other hand* to contrast
  › Order of importance: *most, most important, least, least important, first, finally, mainly, to begin with*
  › Problem and solution: *problem, solution, why, how, solve*
  › Cause-effect: *because, therefore, as a result, cause, effect, so*
  › Chronological order: *first, next, then, finally, before, after, now, in the meantime*

MODEL

During the prewriting stage, the writer of the Student Model understood that his or her argument presented a problem—invasive species—and considered two solutions—to take action against invasive species or to do nothing. The ultimate solution, which the writer expressed in the claim at both the beginning and end of the essay, was that it is up to humans to fix any mess they create, especially the control of invasive species. Therefore, the writer of the Student Model decided that the best approach would be to use a problem-solution organizational structure for the argumentative essay.

At several points in the Student Model, the writer uses cue words or phrases to identify problems and a solution:

But what can be done about this growing ***problem****?*

As a result of the actions of these irresponsible pet owners, Florida is facing a huge ***problem*** *today.*

The ***problem*** *is really complicated, and given the impact on the environment by invasive species (which were introduced by humans in the first place), we humans really must try to restore nature's balance.*

*Despite the difficulties, the only way to **solve** the **problem** is to remove the pythons from the Everglades.*

*In the meantime, the **problem** of invasive species is growing—both ecologically and economically.*

*Although that hunt didn't destroy many pythons, researchers did gather important information about where and how the snakes live, which can help them develop other strategies, but these **solutions** are far into the future.*

*Yet we must try, and we must be part of the **solution.***

Once a writer has selected the most appropriate organizational structure for his or her essay, he or she can use an outline or a graphic organizer (for example, a Venn diagram, flow chart, concept map, or timeline) to begin organizing the supporting evidence.

The writer of the Student Model used a graphic organizer during planning to organize the evidence that supported this claim:

This essay will argue that humans need to take action to solve the problem of invasive species before it's too late to save our native wildlife.

PRACTICE

Use an *Organize Argumentative Writing* graphic organizer such as the one used with the Student Model, or choose one that better suits your organizational pattern. Fill in the organizer with evidence you gathered in the Prewrite stage of writing your argument.

NOTES

SKILL: SUPPORTING DETAILS

DEFINE

An effective argument provides readers with supporting details in the form of reasons and relevant evidence. Reasons are statements that answer the question, "Why?" They tell why the writer thinks that his or her claim is true. The writer provides reasons to support a claim, which makes it more believable. Relevant evidence includes facts, details, statistics, definitions, quotations from experts, observations, and examples. Evidence that supports the reasons and the claim is often found through research.

Research can be the key to presenting a successful argument. While researching, the writer deepens his or her understanding of the topic and finds evidence that supports the reasons and the claim. (Just as important—if the writer can't find enough evidence that supports the claim, then he or she knows it is time to rethink the claim and the reasons.) Without solid supporting evidence, the writer would simply be stating his or her opinion about a topic—and that's rarely convincing to readers.

Because writers want to convince readers that their claims are true, they carefully select and present the supporting details. A detail is relevant only if it supports the claim and helps build the argument. If the detail does not support the claim or strengthen the argument, it is irrelevant and should not be used.

IDENTIFICATION AND APPLICATION

Step 1:

Review your claim. In your research, you want to find supporting details that are relevant to your claim. Ask the following question: "What am I trying to persuade my audience to think or believe?" That's what the writer of the Student Model did. Here's that writer's claim:

This essay will argue that humans need to take action to solve the problem of invasive species before it's too late to save our native wildlife.

Step 2:

Ask what a reader needs to know about the topic in order to accept the claim. For example, to accept a claim about whether to take action against invasive species, a reader must first know the kinds of problems that those invaders are causing. Why are invasive species such a problem? Here's the reason the writer gives:

> **According to a recent online article, "Invasive Species," published by the National Wildlife Federation, "Approximately, 42% of Threatened or Endangered species are at risk primarily due to invasive species" ("Invasive Species" 1).**

That's a reason that should make most readers sit up and pay attention! The writer also provides supporting details that back up that reason. They include a definition and some background information:

- *An invasive non-native species is one that enters a new ecosystem and then settles and reproduces so successfully that it threatens the existence of the area's native species and the balance of the ecosystem itself ("Invasive Species" 1).*
- *These invaders, which may not have any natural predators in the new ecosystem, take over an area, destroying the native wildlife that probably have no defenses against them.*

In the next paragraph, the writer provides another supporting detail—a statistic:

> *According to the research report in this unit, "California Invasive Plant Inventory," approximately 200 non-native invasive plant species are threatening the state's wildlands—"public and private lands that support native ecosystems"—and these plants can "displace native species" and even "alter ecosystem[s]" ("CIPI" 2).*

All of these supporting details came from the writer's research. The details definitely support the writer's claim that invasive species need to be dealt with before something terrible happens.

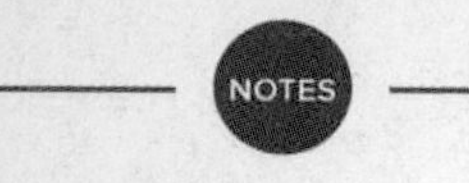

Step 3:

You might find a lot of details in your research, and you might want to use them all to support your claim, but it's important to evaluate each detail before you use it to make sure it's relevant. To do this, ask yourself these questions:

- Does this information help the reader better understand the topic?
- Does this information support my claim?
- Does this information help make my argument believable?
- Do I have stronger evidence that makes the same point?

If you can answer *yes* to the first three questions and *no* to the fourth, then definitely use the supporting detail in your argument.

MODEL

The writer of the Student Model used evidence found during his or her research to support the part of the claim that says that people need to take action now against invasive species.

> In her article "Snakes on the 'Glades," published in *U.S. News & World Report*, Laura Bradley explains that "the Burmese python first arrived in Florida as part of the exotic pet trade, and over time made its way into the Everglades as overwhelmed pet owners released the animals into the wild or they escaped" (Bradley 2). As a result of the actions of these irresponsible pet owners, Florida is facing a huge problem today. According to Michael Sarill, in his blog "Burmese Pythons in the Everglades," **scientists estimate that "anywhere between 30,000 and 150,000 Burmese Pythons exist in South Florida"** (Sarill 1). Because pythons are good at hiding, scientists do not know how many are really out there. Yet according to Sarill, they do know that **the population of native species has declined 90 percent in recent years—including 100 percent for rabbits and some other small mammals (Sarill 1).** Think of the effects of this over time: **The pythons could cause the extinction of every native animal species in the Everglades.** Even the alligators are not safe. Pythons have been known to take on alligators and win (Sarill 3)!

What supporting details does the writer use here? Clearly, the writer provides quotations from experts and statistics about the impact of the Burmese pythons on Florida's native wildlife. This evidence highlights the claim that the

pythons are a deadly threat to Florida's ecosystem, which invites the reader to ask, what can we do?

PRACTICE

Write the claim you developed in a previous lesson. Below it, write some supporting details for your argumentative essay. Use the research you completed earlier in the Extended Writing Project. Then exchange your work with a partner. Use what you've learned about identifying relevant supporting details to evaluate your partner's work. Offer clear suggestions about the kinds of details you, as a reader, would find convincing.

NOTES

PLAN

CA-CCSS: CA.RI.7.1, CA.W.7.1a, CA.W.7.1b, CA.W.7.4, CA.W.7.5, CA.W.7.6, CA.W.7.10, CA.SL.7.1c, CA.SL.7.3

WRITING PROMPT

As you've seen in the short stories and novel and play excerpts in this unit, human interactions are often complicated. Sometimes, we're unaware of the consequences of our actions not only with other humans but also with the environment. For example, what should we do about the "invasive alien species" (sounds like science fiction, doesn't it?) we've introduced into California—species that are threatening the state's native plants and animals? It's your call. Write an argumentative essay in which you explore the challenges caused by human interaction (interference) with the environment. First, reread "California Invasive Plant Inventory" to review the issue of invasive species. Then do research. Choose an invasive plant or animal, such as the Burmese python that people have introduced into the Florida Everglades or kudzu, a spreading invasive plant. Research your invasive plant or animal in at least three print or digital sources, such as books, magazines, or reliable websites. As you research, ask yourself: Should humans try to solve this problem or let nature take its course?

Your argument should include:

- an explicitly stated claim about whether humans should try to clean up the "mess" they started
- persuasive reasons and relevant textual evidence, logically organized
- acknowledgment of opposing claims or other points of view
- citations of your sources in your essay and in a Works Cited page
- a conclusion that restates your claim and summarizes your persuasive evidence

NOTES

Review the organizational structure and information you used to complete your *Organize Argumentative Writing* graphic organizer. This organized information and your claim will help you create a road map to use for writing your argumentative essay.

Consider the following questions as you develop your main paragraph topics and their supporting details in the road map:

- What invasive species is the topic of your essay?
- What claim (or argument) are you making about this invasive species? (Are you for or against taking action against the invader?)
- What are your reasons for making this claim?
- What specific supporting details and relevant evidence from your research can you use to support your claim?
- How can you best present the evidence so that it persuades your audience to accept your claim?

Use this model to get started with your road map:

Argumentative Essay Road Map

Claim: Humans need to take action to solve the problem of invasive species before it's too late to save our native wildlife.

Paragraph 1 (Introduction) Topic: The problem of invasive species

Supporting Detail #1: Make connection to alien invasions from science-fiction movies

Supporting Detail #2: Explain why invasive species are a problem

State the claim.

Paragraph 2 Topic: What an invasive species is

Supporting Detail #1: Quote definition from National Wildlife Federation

Supporting Detail #2: Explain why invasive species are bad, with facts from NWF article

Paragraph 3 Topic: Invasive species in California

Supporting Detail #1: Use statistics from "California Invasive Plant Inventory" to describe situation in California today

Supporting Detail #2: Transition to invasion of Burmese python in Florida Everglades

Paragraph 4 Topic: Invasion of Burmese Python in Florida

Supporting Detail #1: Quote from *U.S. News & World Report* about how pythons arrived in Florida

Supporting Detail #2: Quote statistics from Michael Sarill's blog to illustrate terrible effects of pythons in the Everglades—30,000 to 150,000 pythons, 100% extinction of rabbits

Supporting Detail #3: Prediction of possible effects in the future

Paragraph 5 Topic: Stopping the pythons

Supporting Detail #1: Pose questions about whether people can stop the spread of pythons

Supporting Detail #2: Raise opposing view that we should do nothing because pythons will eventually turn on themselves

Paragraph 6 Topic: Flaws in the do-nothing argument

Supporting Detail #1: Explain why the argument is not reasonable

Supporting Detail #2: Quote from Sarill about dangers to people and rural communities if we do nothing

Supporting Detail #3: Suggest a solution: We must try to restore nature's balance

Paragraph 7 Topic: Solution to the python invasion

Supporting Detail #1: Paraphrase from *U.S. News & World Report* article about 2012 python hunt

Supporting Detail #2: Make point that researchers learned a lot but can't do much

Paragraph 8 (Conclusion) Topic: Summing Up

Supporting Detail #1: Statistics from *U.S. News & World Report* about how much money invasive species cost the U.S. each year

Supporting Detail #2: Make connection between different types of invasive species

Restate the claim.

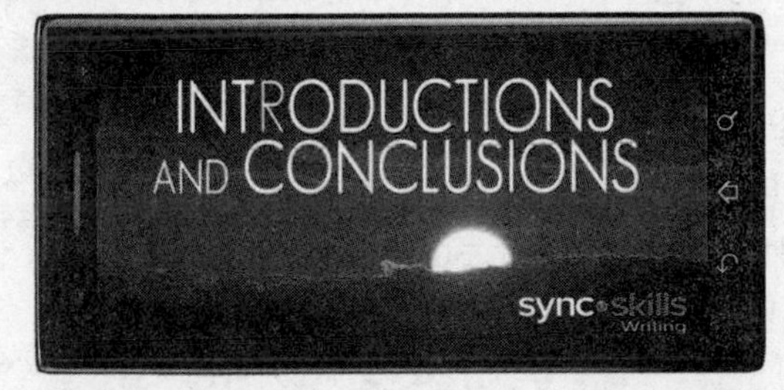

SKILL: INTRODUCTIONS AND CONCLUSIONS

NOTES

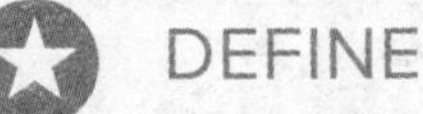

DEFINE

The introduction is the opening paragraph or section of an argumentative essay or another nonfiction text. The introduction of an argumentative essay identifies the topic to be discussed, states the writer's claim, and previews the supporting details (reasons and evidence found during research) that will appear in the body of the text. The introduction is also the place where most writers include a "hook" that engages readers and helps them relate to the topic.

A conclusion is the closing paragraph or section of an argumentative essay or another type of nonfiction text. The conclusion is where the writer brings the argument to a close. The ideas presented in the conclusion follow directly from the claim stated in the introduction and from the supporting details provided in the body of the argument. Therefore, the conclusion is where the writer restates the claim and summarizes his or her evidence and research. Also, the conclusion of an argument might end with a call to action or an insightful comment that will leave the reader with something to think about.

IDENTIFICATION AND APPLICATION

- In an argument, the introduction is the opening section in which the writer identifies the topic to be discussed and directly states the claim. The claim expresses the writer's opinion (or point of view) about the topic. By presenting the claim at the beginning of the argument, the writer lets readers know his or her position on the topic. This allows readers to form their own opinions, which they can then measure against the writer's as they read the supporting details in the body of the argument—the middle of the essay.
- The introduction is also where the writer provides a preview of the supporting evidence. By providing a preview, the writer can begin to establish an effective argument and increase the likelihood that readers will accept and agree with his or her claim.

- The introduction should also have a "hook." As the word implies, a good hook "grabs" the reader's interest and makes him or her want to read on. A good hook might consist of an intriguing image, a surprising detail, a funny anecdote, a rhetorical question, or a shocking statistic.
- An effective conclusion restates the writer's claim and briefly summarizes the most convincing reasons and researched evidence from the body paragraphs in the essay.
- Some conclusions may offer a compelling insight related to the argument. This insight is the writer's last chance to persuade the audience to accept his or her side of the argument and may even inspire the audience to take action. The insight might be
  - › an answer to a question first posed in the introduction.
  - › a memorable or inspiring message or quotation.
  - › a suggestion that readers learn more.

The introduction and conclusion of the Student Model "What Do We Do About Invasive Species?" contains many of the key elements discussed above:

> **How many science-fiction movies have you seen about alien invasions from Mars or elsewhere and the effects that these alien invaders have had on the people and places on Earth?** But as the saying goes, truth is often stranger than fiction, and today, humans are facing a real alien invasion, except this time the invaders are not extraterrestrials in the usual sense. **They are invasive alien plants and animals that humans have thoughtlessly introduced into areas where they do not belong.** What is the effect of this harmful human activity? Nothing less than the extinction of many of the world's native wildlife! **But what can be done about this growing problem? Should humans be forced to clean up the mess they started?** Or should humans do nothing and let nature take its course? These are the two sides of the issue. **This essay will argue that humans need to take action to solve the problem of invasive species before it's too late to save our native wildlife.** The question is, how? But first, let's look at the issue.

The student writer's introductory paragraph **"hooks"** readers by referring to alien invasions in science-fiction movies. The hook is fun and would likely appeal to the writer's classmates, who are his or her most likely audience. The writer moves from imaginary alien invaders to real invasive species, which is the essay's **topic.** By posing a few questions, the writer helps **preview information and details** that he or she will discuss in the body of the essay. Finally, the writer ends the introduction with the **claim,** or statement of opinion:

NOTES

> "... humans need to take action to solve the problem of invasive species before it's too late to save our native wildlife."

Now let's look at how the writer ended the argumentative essay:

> In the meantime, the problem of invasive species is growing—both ecologically and economically. According to Bradley, **the nation "spends more than $120 billion each year dealing with 50,000 introduced species of plants, animals, and microbes"** (Bradley 1–2). **If we can't control 18-foot-long, 200-pound pythons, how can we even begin to fight against thousands of microbes?** Yet we must try, and we must be part of the solution. We humans have had both a positive and negative impact on our environment. **When we make a mistake, such as releasing a dangerous predator like the Burmese python into the wild, we must do everything we can to make things right.**

The concluding paragraph does a few important things:

- First, it **reviews the topic**—invasive species are a big and growing problem.
- It **states some final and compelling evidence**—that the U.S. spends billions of dollars each year trying to control invasive species.
- It **asks a question** for the purpose of getting the reader to think about the seriousness of the issue: "If we can't control 18-foot-long, 200-pound pythons, how can we even begin to fight against thousands of microbes?"
- Finally, it **restates the claim:** "When we make a mistake, such as releasing a dangerous predator like the Burmese python into the wild, we must do everything we can to make things right."
- A concluding paragraph should also **restate the most important reasons and evidence** presented in the body of the essay. That's something the writer of the Student Model needs to work on during revision.

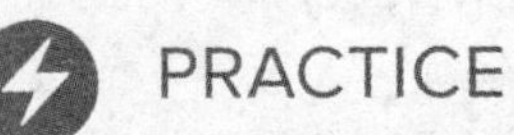

PRACTICE

Write an introduction and a conclusion to your argument. Your introduction should include a "hook," identify your topic, state your claim, and hint at the supporting details (reasons and evidence from your research) that will appear in the body of your essay. Then draft a conclusion that mirrors your introduction by restating your claim and summing up your research. Try to include an insightful comment or interesting question about your topic or claim. Finally, exchange your work with a peer-review partner. Provide helpful feedback about each other's introduction and conclusion.

NOTES

SKILL: BODY PARAGRAPHS AND TRANSITIONS

DEFINE

Body paragraphs appear between the introduction and conclusion of an argumentative essay, or any type of nonfiction text. Together, they form the middle section in which the writer of the argument supports his or her claim with relevant reasons and evidence collected during research. Ideally, each body paragraph should focus on one central idea or reason so that the reader can easily follow along. The ideas in each body paragraph should support the claim stated in the introduction and restated in the conclusion.

It's important to structure a body paragraph clearly. Here is one way to structure the body paragraph of an argumentative essay:

- **Topic sentence:** The topic sentence is the first sentence of a body paragraph. It states the central idea of the paragraph. The topic sentence should relate to your claim.
- **Evidence #1:** You should provide evidence that supports your topic sentence. Evidence can include relevant facts, definitions, details, observations, quotations, statistics, and examples.
- **Evidence #2:** Continue to develop your claim with a second piece of evidence.
- **Analysis/Explanation:** After presenting evidence, explain how the evidence helps support your topic sentence—and general claim—about the topic.
- **Concluding sentence:** After presenting your evidence and analysis, restate your claim or main point in a concluding sentence.

As you write body paragraphs, think carefully about how to incorporate your evidence. **Quotations** are an excellent source of evidence, but they need to be integrated into your writing. Be sure to introduce the source of the quotation before you quote it, and place the exact words of the quotations within quotation marks. End the sentence with a citation, so that readers know the source of the quoted material.

NOTES

Compare these examples of a poorly integrated and a well-integrated quotation:

> **Poorly integrated quotation:** Laura Bradley wrote an article "Snakes on the 'Glades," which appeared in *U.S. News & World Report.* In it she said that "the Burmese python first arrived in Florida as part of the exotic pet trade, and over time made its way into the Everglades as overwhelmed pet owners released the animals into the wild or they escaped" (Bradley 2).

> **Well-integrated quotation:** In her article "Snakes on the 'Glades," published in *U.S. News & World Report,* Laura Bradley explains that " the Burmese python first arrived in Florida as part of the exotic pet trade, and over time made its way into the Everglades as overwhelmed pet owners released the animals into the wild or they escaped" (Bradley 2).

Remember, if a full quotation is too long, you can use **ellipses** (. . .) to show that you left out some words:

> The problem is really complicated, and given the impact on the environment by invasive species (which were introduced by humans in the first place), we humans really must try to restore nature's balance.

> The problem is really complicated, and given the impact on the environment by invasive species . . . we humans must really try to restore nature's balance.

If a quotation is too long or too complicated, you can **paraphrase** it—or any of your evidence. Paraphrasing involves restating the key ideas by using your own words. Here's an example:

> According to Michael Sarill, in his blog "Burmese Pythons in the Everglades," scientists estimate that "anywhere between 30,000 and 150,000 Burmese Pythons exist in South Florida" (Sarill 1). Because pythons are good at hiding, scientists do not know how many are really out there. Yet according to Sarill, they do know that the population of native species has declined 90 percent in recent years—including 100 percent for rabbits and some other small mammals (Sarill 1). Think of the effects of this over time: The pythons could cause the extinction of every native animal species in the Everglades. Even the alligators are not safe. Pythons have been known to take on alligators and win (Sarill 3)!

According to Michael Sarill, scientists estimate that perhaps 30,000 to 150,000 Burmese Pythons exist in South Florida (Sarill 1). As a result, the population of native species has dropped by 90 percent or more (Sarill 1). Think about what that could mean over time: The pythons could cause every native animal species in the Everglades to become extinct—even the alligators (Sarill 3)!

Transitions such as *and, but,* or *or* help writers make connections between words in a sentence, while words and phrases such as *also, in addition to,* and *likewise* help writers establish relationships between ideas in body paragraphs. Transitions help make connections between words in a sentence and ideas in individual paragraphs. Adding transition words or phrases like these to the beginning or end of a paragraph can help a writer guide readers smoothly through a text.

IDENTIFICATION AND APPLICATION

- Body paragraphs are the middle paragraphs that come between the introduction and the conclusion. In an argumentative essay, these paragraphs provide reasons and supporting evidence and focus on one central idea for each body paragraph.
  - A topic sentence clearly states the central idea of a body paragraph.
  - Evidence consists of facts, definitions, quotations, statistics, and examples.
  - Analysis explains how the evidence supports the topic sentence and the claim.
  - A concluding sentence wraps up the central (or main) idea of the paragraph.

- Certain transition words and phrases, such as *for example,* can show the relationship between a main point and its evidence, but transitions can also indicate the organizational structure of a text. Here are some examples:
  - Cause-effect: *because, since, as a result, so, since, therefore, if . . . then*
  - Compare and contrast: *like, also, both, in the same way,* to show comparison and *although, while, but, yet, still, however, on the contrary,* to indicate contrast
  - Chronological (or time) order: *first, next, then, finally, soon, in a few years*

NOTES

- Quotations are an excellent source of evidence. You can use direct quotes from sources, or you can paraphrase a quote in your own words. To avoid plagiarism, be sure to introduce the source of the quotation before you quote it.
  - › Place the exact words of the quotation within quotation marks.
  - › Whenever you paraphrase or provide a direct quote, end the sentence with a citation so that readers know the source of the words or ideas.

MODEL

The Student Model uses a body paragraph structure to develop the claim. It also includes transitions to help the reader understand the relationship between (or among) ideas and to indicate the text's organizational structure.

Read the second body paragraph from the Student Model "What Do We Do About Invasive Alien Species?" Look closely at the structure and think about how the writer incorporated his or her research. Notice the transition words in bold. How effective is the paragraph's structure? Does it develop ideas related to the claim? How do the transition words and phrases help you understand the text's organizational structure and the relationships between (or among) ideas?

> *Unfortunately, many examples of alien species invasions exist today across the United States. According to the research report in this unit, "California Invasive Plant Inventory," approximately 200 non-native invasive plant species are threatening the state's wildlands—"public and private lands that support native ecosystems," and these plants can "displace native species" and even "alter ecosystem[s]" ("CIPI" 2).* ***Although*** *these invasive plant species pose a danger to California's wildlands, perhaps no greater threat by an invasive species exists today than that of the Burmese python in the Florida Everglades.*

The **topic sentence** of this paragraph refers back to the **claim,** which argues that invasive species are a big problem. The sentence is immediately followed by **evidence** in the form of a **quotation** that contains a statistic and a definition. The writer neatly **integrates** the quotation and introduces it by identifying the source. Next follows some analysis. The writer explains that although the threat from invasive species is bad in California, it is worse in Florida. The **transition** word *although* indicates the contrast. This sentence is also the **concluding sentence** of the paragraph and clearly broadcasts to readers that the next paragraph of the argumentative essay will focus on the invasion of the Burmese python in the Florida Everglades.

PRACTICE

Write the body paragraphs of your essay following the format above. Then choose a paragraph to edit. Make sure you have used clear transitions, and check that you have integrated your research smoothly and correctly. When you have finished, exchange work with a partner. Offer each other feedback by answering the following questions:

- How accurate is the topic sentence? Does it state what the paragraph is about? Does it refer to the claim?
- How strong is the evidence used to support the topic sentence?
- Are all quotes and paraphrases integrated well and cited properly?
- Does the evidence thoroughly support the topic sentence—and the claim?
- Does the paragraph include analysis?
- How effective is the concluding sentence?

NOTES

DRAFT

CA-CCSS: CA.RI.7.1, CA.RI.7.6, CA.RI.7.8, CA.W.7.1a, CA.W.7.1b, CA.W.7.1c, CA.W.7.1d, CA.W.7.1e, CA.W.7.4, CA.W.7.5, CA.W.7.6, CA.W.7.8, CA.W.7.9b, CA.W.7.10, CA.SL.7.1a, CA.SL.7.1b, CA.SL.7.1c, CA.SL.7.1d, CA.SL.7.3, CA.L.7.1a, CA.L.7.6

WRITING PROMPT

As you've seen in the short stories and novel and play excerpts in this unit, human interactions are often complicated. Sometimes, we're unaware of the consequences of our actions not only with other humans but also with the environment. For example, what should we do about the "invasive alien species" (sounds like science fiction, doesn't it?) we've introduced into California—species that are threatening the state's native plants and animals? It's your call. Write an argumentative essay in which you explore the challenges caused by human interaction (interference) with the environment. First, reread "California Invasive Plant Inventory" to review the issue of invasive species. Then do research. Choose an invasive plant or animal, such as the Burmese python that people have introduced into the Florida Everglades or kudzu, a spreading invasive plant. Research your invasive plant or animal in at least three print or digital sources, such as books, magazines, or reliable websites. As you research, ask yourself: Should humans try to solve this problem or let nature take its course?

Your argument should include:

- an explicitly stated claim about whether humans should try to clean up the "mess" they started
- persuasive reasons and relevant textual evidence, logically organized
- acknowledgment of opposing claims or other points of view
- citations of your sources in your essay and in a Works Cited page
- a conclusion that restates your claim and summarizes your persuasive evidence

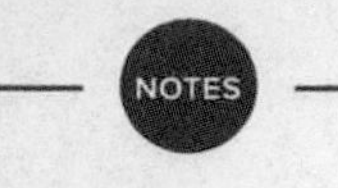

You've already begun working on your own argumentative essay. So far, you've thought about your purpose, audience, and topic. You've researched invasive species and the problems they cause. You've also researched possible solutions, so you should have some solid evidence that supports your claim, or thesis statement, by now. You've decided how to organize your argument and have gathered supporting details in the form of reasons and relevant evidence. You've also thought about and begun to write an introduction, body paragraphs, and a conclusion. What's left to do? It's time to put all your hard work together to write a draft of your argumentative essay.

Use your road map and your other prewriting and planning materials to help you as you write. Remember that an argument begins with an introduction that contains your explicitly stated claim. Body paragraphs then develop your claim by providing supporting details—your reasons and relevant evidence, such as facts, statistics, quotations from experts, and examples. These middle paragraphs also contain an analysis of your evidence, and they include transitions. These transition words and phrases help your readers recognize your organizational structure and the connections between (or among) your ideas. Your concluding paragraph restates or reinforces your claim and summarizes the important points from the argument you've made. Your conclusion may also contain your strongest argument, and it may leave your readers with something intriguing to think about.

When drafting your argumentative essay, ask yourself these questions:

- How effective is my introduction? Will my "hook" grab my reader's interest?
- How can I express my claim more clearly? Will readers understand which side I'm on?
- Which relevant evidence from my research—including facts, quotations, statistics, and examples—best supports my claim?
- How can I use transitions to improve the structure and flow of my argument?
- How well have I integrated quotations and paraphrases from my research into the body of my essay?
- How convincing are my reasons and evidence?
- How effectively do I restate my claim in the conclusion?
- Have I left my readers with something to think about?

Be sure to read your draft closely before you submit it. You want to make sure that you've addressed every part of the prompt.

NOTES

SKILL: SOURCES AND CITATIONS

DEFINE

As you have learned, sources are the texts that writers use to research their writing. A primary source is a firsthand account of events by the person who experienced them. Another type of source is known as a secondary source. This is a source that analyzes or interprets primary sources. Citations are notes that provide information about the source texts. It is necessary for a writer to provide a citation if he or she quotes directly from a text or refers to someone else's ideas. The citation lets readers know who stated the quoted words or originally came up with the idea.

IDENTIFICATION AND APPLICATION

- Sources can be either primary or secondary. Primary sources are firsthand accounts or original materials, such as the following:
  - Letters or other correspondence
  - Photographs
  - Official documents
  - Diaries or journals
  - Autobiographies or memoirs
  - Eyewitness accounts and interviews
  - Audio recordings and radio broadcasts
  - Literary texts, such as novels, poems, fables, and dramas
  - Works of art
  - Artifacts
  - Scientific lab reports and study results
- Secondary sources are usually texts. They are the written interpretation and analysis of primary source materials. Some examples of secondary sources include:
  - Encyclopedia articles
  - Textbooks

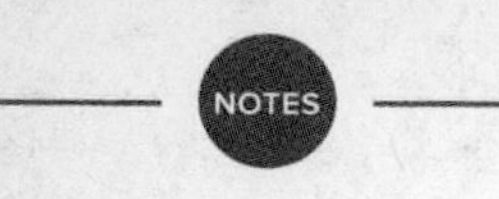

- › Histories
- › Documentary films
- › News analyses
- › Science books and articles

- Whether sources are primary or secondary, they must be **credible** and **accurate.** This means the information in the sources should be reliable.
- When a writer quotes directly from a source, he or she must copy the words exactly as they appear in the source, placing them within quotation marks. Here's an example from the Student Model:

 According to a recent online article, "Invasive Species," published by the National Wildlife Federation, "Approximately, 42% of Threatened or Endangered species are at risk primarily due to invasive species" ("Invasive Species" 1).

- Writers must cite the sources they're quoting directly. One way to do this is by putting the author's name (or the title, if there is no author) in parentheses at the end of the sentence and the page number on which the quotation appears. Another method is to cite the author's name or source title in the sentence. In the example above from the Student Model, the writer does both because the citation in parentheses does not make clear who actually said the quoted words.
- Writers must also provide citations when borrowing ideas from another source, even when writers are just paraphrasing, or putting the ideas into their own words. Citations serve to credit the source and help readers find out where they can learn more. Furthermore, they help writers avoid **plagiarizing,** or presenting the words and ideas of someone else as their own.
- There are several different styles for citations. Ask your teacher to identify the style he or she prefers.
- Writers who cite sources in the body of their writing need to provide a **Works Cited** section that lists all the sources the writer used. As with citations, there are different styles of Works Cited lists, but the sources are always listed in alphabetical order, by author's last name, or, if the source has no author, then by the title.

MODEL

In this excerpt from the Student Model "What Do We Do About Invasive Alien Species?" the writer quotes from two different sources and identifies each source.

NOTES

In her article "Snakes on the 'Glades," published online in *U.S. News & World Report,* Laura Bradley explains that **"the Burmese python first arrived in Florida as part of the exotic pet trade, and over time made its way into the Everglades as overwhelmed pet owners released the animals into the wild or they escaped"** (Bradley 2). As a result of the actions of these irresponsible pet owners, Florida is facing a huge problem today. According to Michael Sarill, in his blog "Burmese Pythons in the Everglades," scientists estimate that **"anywhere between 30,000 and 150,000 Burmese Pythons exist in South Florida"** (Sarill 1). Because pythons are good at hiding, scientists do not know how many are really out there. **Yet according to Sarill, they do know that the population of native species has declined 90 percent in recent years—including 100 percent for rabbits and some other small mammals (Sarill 1).** Think of the effects of this over time: **The pythons could cause the extinction of every native animal species in the Everglades. Even the alligators are not safe. Pythons have been known to take on alligators and win (Sarill 3)!**

Notice that only the portions of text taken directly from the source appear in quotations. Paraphrased information should not appear within quotation marks but still must be cited. In each case, the author's last name and the page number on which the information appears are placed in parentheses after the sentence that contains the quoted or paraphrased material.

Here is how the writer's sources appear in the Works Cited section that follows the argumentative essay:

Works Cited

Bradley, Laura. "Snakes on the 'Glades." *U.S. News & World Report* 21 July 2014. Web. **9 Dec. 2014. <http://www.usnews.com/news/articles/2014/07/21/invasive-pythons-threaten-florida-everglades>**

California Invasive Plant Council. "California Invasive Plant Inventory." 2006. Print.

"Invasive Species." National Wildlife Federation. **Web. 9 Dec. 2014** <http://www.nwf.org/wildlife/threats-to-wildlife/invasive-species.aspx>

Sarill, Michael. "Burmese Pythons in the Everglades." *Baboon* 12 Sept. 2013. Web. **9 Dec. 2014.** <http://www.baboongame.com/blog/burmese-pythons-everglades#.VIc9NVrgA1Q>

Notice how the sources are listed alphabetically by the author's last name, or if the source has no author, then by the title. The author's name is followed by the title of the piece, and the title is followed by the publication information. When the writer uses a source published online, the writer needs to identify its URL and give the date of when he or she accessed it. From this Works Cited section, you can tell that the writer accessed three of the online sources on the same day.

PRACTICE

If you have not yet written your Works Cited section, you can do that now. Go back to your draft and check that you have cited your sources correctly. Edit your citations, making sure they follow the conventions your teacher recommended. Then exchange your Works Cited section with a partner and provide each other with feedback. Look carefully at how your partner alphabetized, formatted, and punctuated the citations. Edit and provide constructive feedback.

NOTES

REVISE

CA-CCSS: CA.RI.7.8, CA.W.7.1a, CA.W.7.1b, CA.W.7.1c, CA.W.7.1d, CA.W.7.1e, CA.W.7.4, CA.W.7.5, CA.W.7.6, CA.W.7.8, CA.W.7.9b, CA.W.7.10, CA.SL.7.1a, CA.SL.7.1b, CA.SL.7.1c, CA.SL.7.1d, CA.SL.7.3, CA.L.7.1a, CA.L.7.1b, CA.L.7.1c, CA.L.7.3a

WRITING PROMPT

As you've seen in the short stories and novel and play excerpts in this unit, human interactions are often complicated. Sometimes, we're unaware of the consequences of our actions not only with other humans but also with the environment. For example, what should we do about the "invasive alien species" (sounds like science fiction, doesn't it?) we've introduced into California—species that are threatening the state's native plants and animals? It's your call. Write an argumentative essay in which you explore the challenges caused by human interaction (interference) with the environment. First, reread "California Invasive Plant Inventory" to review the issue of invasive species. Then do research. Choose an invasive plant or animal, such as the Burmese python that people have introduced into the Florida Everglades or kudzu, a spreading invasive plant. Research your invasive plant or animal in at least three print or digital sources, such as books, magazines, or reliable websites. As you research, ask yourself: Should humans try to solve this problem or let nature take its course?

Your argument should include:

- an explicitly stated claim about whether humans should try to clean up the "mess" they started
- persuasive reasons and relevant textual evidence, logically organized
- acknowledgment of opposing claims or other points of view
- citations of your sources in your essay and in a Works Cited page
- a conclusion that restates your claim and summarizes your persuasive evidence

You have written a draft of your argumentative essay. You have also received feedback from your peers about how to improve it. Now you are going to revise your draft.

Here are some recommendations to help you revise:

- Review the suggestions made by your peers. You don't have to incorporate every suggestion, but you should carefully consider each one.
- Remember to maintain a formal style. A formal style is appropriate for your purpose—persuading readers to agree with your ideas about a topic. It is also appropriate for your audience—students, teachers, family members, and other readers interested in learning more about your topic.
  - › Use standard English in your writing. As you revise, eliminate any informal language, particularly slang, unless it is included in quoted material or is essential to readers' understanding.
  - › Review your language. Look for the most persuasive language you can use.
  - › Check that you have placed phrases and clauses correctly in each sentence. Now that you know how to use adjective clauses, make sure that you place them logically when you combine sentences.
  - › Look for and correct any dangling modifiers by revising a few words. See the following example:
    - › **Unclear:** Having finished her homework, a snack was needed.
    - › **Corrected:** Having finished her homework, Carla needed a snack.
  - › Fix any misplaced modifiers by rearranging your words. See the following example:
    - › **Unclear:** Ted ran for the bus in his raincoat, which was ten minutes late.
    - › **Correct:** Ted ran in his raincoat for the bus, which was ten minutes late.
  - › Incorporate sentence variety in your writing. Check that you aren't beginning every sentence in the same way. Try for a mix of simple, compound, complex, and compound-complex sentences. This will create an interesting structure that will keep readers engaged in your writing.

- After you have revised for elements of style, use these questions to review your argument for how you could improve its organization and supporting details:
  - › How explicitly have you stated your claim in the introduction? Could you revise your claim, or thesis statement, to make your position clearer to your readers?

NOTES

- Is your organizational structure clear? Is it the best choice for your argument? Would your argument flow better if you used more or different transitions?
- Do you need to add more evidence such as quotations, facts, examples, statistics, or other data to support your claim? Are you missing supporting details that could help your readers better understand your ideas?
- How well have you incorporated your research into your sentences and paragraphs?
- Are your quotations clearly introduced and punctuated properly?
- Have you double-checked your citations to make sure you have correctly cited the source of the quote in the body of the essay and in the Works Cited section of the paper?

EDIT, PROOFREAD, AND PUBLISH

CA-CCSS: CA.W.7.1a, CA.W.7.1b, CA.W.7.1c, CA.W.7.1d, CA.W.7.1e, CA.W.7.4, CA.W.7.5, CA.W.7.6, CA.W.7.8, CA.W.7.9b, CA.W.7.10, CA.SL.7.1c, CA.SL.7.1d, CA.SL.7.3, CA.SL.7.6, CA.L.7.1a, CA.L.7.1b, CA.L.7.1c, CA.L.7.2a, CA.L.7.2b, CA.L.7.3a, CA.L.7.4b, CA.L.7.4c, CA.L.7.6

WRITING PROMPT

As you've seen in the short stories and novel and play excerpts in this unit, human interactions are often complicated. Sometimes, we're unaware of the consequences of our actions not only with other humans but also with the environment. For example, what should we do about the "invasive alien species" (sounds like science fiction, doesn't it?) we've introduced into California—species that are threatening the state's native plants and animals? It's your call. Write an argumentative essay in which you explore the challenges caused by human interaction (interference) with the environment. First, reread "California Invasive Plant Inventory" to review the issue of invasive species. Then do research. Choose an invasive plant or animal, such as the Burmese python that people have introduced into the Florida Everglades or kudzu, a spreading invasive plant. Research your invasive plant or animal in at least three print or digital sources, such as books, magazines, or reliable websites. As you research, ask yourself: Should humans try to solve this problem or let nature take its course?

Your argument should include:

- an explicitly stated claim about whether humans should try to clean up the "mess" they started
- persuasive reasons and relevant textual evidence, logically organized
- acknowledgment of opposing claims or other points of view
- citations of your sources in your essay and in a Works Cited page
- a conclusion that restates your claim and summarizes your persuasive evidence

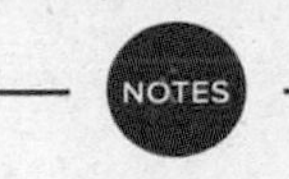

Now that you've revised your argumentative essay and received feedback from your peers, it's time to edit and proofread your essay to produce a final version. Ask yourself these questions:

- Have I thought about the suggestions from my peers?
- Have I fully supported my claim with strong evidence from my research?
- Have I incorporated my research and cited my sources correctly?
- Would the organizational flow of my argument benefit from more transitions?
- What else can I do to improve my argument and its organization?

Once you are satisfied with the content of your work, proofread it for errors in capitalization, punctuation, grammar, and spelling. Ask yourself these questions:

- Have I used capitalization correctly for names and titles of works?
- Have I placed direct quotations within quotation marks?
- Have I used the proper punctuation for my print and online citations?
- Have I used commas correctly to separate coordinate adjectives in my sentences?
- Have I used commas correctly to separate dependent and independent clauses in compound, complex, and compound-complex sentences?
- Have I corrected any mistakes in grammar or usage?
- Have I checked my spelling and corrected any misspelled words?

PHOTO/IMAGE CREDITS:

Cover, ©iStock.com/-aniaostudio-, ©iStock.com/Gannet77, ©iStock.com/alexey_boldin, ©iStock.com/skegbydave
p. iii, ©iStock.com/DNY59, ©iStock.com/alexey_boldin, ©iStockphoto.com, ©iStock.com/Massonstock
p. iv, ©iStockphoto.com/Urs Siedentop
p. vii, ©iStock.com/moevin, ©iStock.com/skegbydave, ©iStock.com/Chemlamp, ©iStock.com/svariophoto
p. 2, ©iStock.com/-aniaostudio-
p. 4, ©iStock.com/THEPALMER
p. 9, ©iStock.com/francisblack
p. 17, ©iStock.com/melissasanger
p. 25, ©iStock.com/mammuth
p. 33, ©iStock/Viktor_Gladkov
p. 45, ©iStock.com/lolostock
p. 52, ©iStock.com/alexey05
p. 59, ©iStock.com/kali9
p. 65, ©iStock.com/ImagineGolf
p. 72, ©iStock.com/bybostanci
p. 79, ©iStock.com/wwing
p. 91, ©iStock.com/DenisZbukarev
p. 97, ©iStock.com/SHSPhotography
p. 105, ©iStock.com/stanley45
p. 114, ©iStock.com/moevin, ©iStock.com/svariophoto
p. 115, ©iStock.com/moevin, ©iStock.com/skegbydave
p. 121, ©iStock.com/moevin, ©iStock.com/skegbydave
p. 125, ©iStock.com/DNY59, ©iStock.com/skegbydave
p. 129, ©iStock.com/Chemlamp, ©iStock.com/skegbydave
p. 131, ©iStock.com/THEPALMER, ©iStock.com/skegbydave
p. 134, ©iStock.com/shaunl, ©iStock.com/skegbydave
p. 138, ©iStock.com/moevin, ©iStock.com/skegbydave
p. 141, ©iStock.com/alephx01, ©iStock.com/skegbydave
p. 144, ©iStock.com/Jeff_Hu, ©iStock.com/skegbydave
p. 149, ©iStock.com/moevin, ©iStock.com/skegbydave
p. 151, ©iStock.com/mmac72, ©iStock.com/skegbydave
p. 155, ©iStock.com/moevin, ©iStock.com/skegbydave
p. 158, ©iStock.com/moevin, ©iStock.com/skegbydave

Text Fulfillment Through StudySync

If you are interested in specific titles, please fill out the form below and we will check availability through our partners.

ORDER DETAILS

Date:

TITLE	AUTHOR	Paperback/ Hardcover	Specific Edition *If Applicable*	Quantity

SHIPPING INFORMATION

Contact:
Title:
School/District:
Address Line 1:
Address Line 2:
Zip or Postal Code:
Phone:
Mobile:
Email:

BILLING INFORMATION

☐ *SAME AS SHIPPING*

Contact:
Title:
School/District:
Address Line 1:
Address Line 2:
Zip or Postal Code:
Phone:
Mobile:
Email:

PAYMENT INFORMATION

☐ CREDIT CARD

Name on Card:

Card Number: Expiration Date: Security Code:

☐ PO

Purchase Order Number:

StudySync Text Fulfillment, BookheadEd Learning, LLC
610 Daniel Young Drive | Sonoma, CA 95476